SOMETIMES I CRY IN THE SHOWER

A GRIEVING FATHER'S JOURNEY TO WHOLENESS AND HEALING

R. GLENN KELLY

SOMETIMES I CRY IN THE SHOWER

CONTENTS

Dedication

To my loving son, Jonathan, whose life touched so many who were blessed to know him...And so many others who did not.

I will see you again one day, my angel. Until then, I will honor the legacy you left behind for me...always.

PREFACE

Breathe. Listen for my footfall in your heart.
I am not gone but merely walk within you.

~Nicholas Evans

Who am I? I am a father who experienced the unimaginable, heart-rending loss of my beautiful, beloved son, Jonathan. From the moment of birth, that miracle child transformed his father from a self-centered, non-spiritual man into the hero in his son's eye. Unexpectedly, Jonathan would be taken from me after sixteen years when his heart of gold failed after a relatively routine medical procedure.

Who am I? I am someone raised by strong loving parents, along with the most incredible, non-judgmental brothers and sisters. I am someone who moved into adulthood volunteering for a life of serving my country and then my community. I am someone whose life was pretty much on autopilot and who had every expectation that nothing so tragic would ever find its way into my life. It did.

Who I am now is a grieving father on a journey towards healing. However, I do not expect or really want to "heal" completely, as there are parts of pain within loss that I never want to stop hurting. No parent should ever outlive his or her child. Who I am now, however, is someone with an incredible sense of personal peace discovered only during my journey of self-awareness, which began after my child and best friend came back to me in spirit in order that I recall the legacy he left behind for his father. Because of that, who I am now is someone with an empty place in his heart that yet takes joy in the knowledge I can go on with life and look forward to seeing my beautiful boy again someday.

Who I am not is a doctor or psychiatrist. I am not someone with a psychology education or formal training in grief counseling. Truth be told, I have not even attended counseling myself. I am neither hyper-intelligent nor more open to spiritualism than most. I am just someone openly willing to share my travails before my loss, as well as the trek to healing afterwards. If you are a grieving father, or the loved one or friend seeking to understand the possible aftermath of a dreadful, unimaginable loss, you may have already found little support for men. I am merely someone who wants to share my story and findings with other grieving fathers who, possibly in the quiet solitude of a corner chair, might read of my personal enlightenment and realize you are not alone. We can be, and above all else, must be fine again, as we have so much to live and so much to give. This publication is actually one of my many steps in seeking wholeness and I cannot thank you enough for walking beside me on a path of healing.

I have never met a strong man who had an easy past.

The Shower

"It is such a secret place, the land of tears."
~Antoine de Saint-Exupéry, The Little Prince

The spattering of water gratefully mutes the outside world. Here in this oblong tub of glossy, white ceramic, barely six-feet long by three feet wide, is where my mind chases lofty notions or unwittingly discovers previously unknown answers to life's little struggles. Tucked away in the secluded corner upstairs, the shower curtain may as well be made of steel and the bathroom door of blast proof concrete. The warmth of the water spreads over my shoulders and down my back, creating a welcome exodus from mental constraint, along with its selfish need for guided thought. The shower is my escape. It is my Secret Garden, completely impenetrable to all others where I surprisingly resolve irksome job related troubles, unexpectedly develop the perfect idea for my next wood working project, or find myself with those little epiphanies that make one mumble, "Why didn't I think of that before?" Left in the massaging jets long enough I could probably invent the elusive warp drive for light speed travel, figure out how to get toothpaste back in the tube, or even plot the ultimate scheme for world domination. It is a darned good thing I have chosen to use my showers for good instead of evil. The hot streams of water and the warm, humid air that fills my lungs gives another opportunity for a few minutes of morning meditation. Yet, unlike the thirty minutes of conventional meditation I try to set aside each day to clear my mind, here in my watery "Fortress of Solitude" I do not follow the traditions of shutting out thought altogether. Instead, I delight in the fact that I can stand under the hot flow of water and allow my freshly awakened mind to go simply where it dares.

As my thoughts run freely and uninhibited through the playground in my mind, I also occasionally break down and cry as well. Yes, this former Marine, cop and Alpha male wanna-be openly admits that sometimes I cry in the shower. I have that right, you know. After all, I am a grieving father who did experience the horrendous and life-altering nightmare of losing a child. My wonderful son, Jonathan, who lived for sixteen and a half years, unexpectedly passed away in June of 2013 after what should have been a relatively routine medical procedure. So yeah, I weep and sob in the shower where no one will hear me. In my little second story refuge, with the door shut and curtain drawn, I can let go and tell God I am angry and confused about the greater plan. I can ask Him why he took my son so early in life while I bawl uncontrollably in the noisy spray without anyone questioning either my faith or my manhood. I can lay my palms on the wet tiles on either side of the shower nozzle, look to the heavens with tears and warm water cascading down my face and beg, plead and even offer to trade my very soul to bring my son back. None of that works, of course, but only God, Jonathan and I know I am crying. Does it make me feel better? It absolutely does. Along my path to healing, I would become aware of just how destructive my instincts to hold back those very corrosive emotions can be. Left pent up inside, the caustic nature of unhealthy emotions would have almost certainly changed me into a man I do not want to become. Will I need to cry in the shower in the future? Man, I hope so. By the way, do not gasp. God is okay that I questioned Him and got angry. He certainly gets it.

Please do not think of me as a heartless, stoic man, however, as I often openly wept for the loss of Jonathan in front of others. Early on, it was simply not possible to choke back the lump in my throat while comforted by close family and friends while they recounted the many wonderful virtues of Jonathan. However, I would not and could not fully expose my deep hurt before them. Surely, as a grieving father I would have been fully justified in uncontrollable gushes of anguish and heartache which flow only with the unhindered feelings of desolation, sadness, anger and remorse. Further, I cannot think of a single person who would have blamed me if I had assumed a fetal position in a dark corner that terrible day and remained there until the world just went away. I felt helpless and confused, with a dark emptiness inside that had no name. Because of who I am, however, those emotions could not come out in front of others, and sadly, as the days passed I also hid them from myself.

It is certainly not my intention to say it is wrong or unacceptable for a man grieving with the pain of child loss to express his emotions in front of others. Actually, it absolutely would be the right thing to do, if only he can. If I had been able to do that from the start, I would have certainly gained a pretty good head start on dealing with some real demons that hung around for quite some time afterwards. Immediately after the loss of Jonathan, I would not openly express my raw, angry, and empty feelings no matter how hard they tore at my heart and soul. I am aware, however, that even if I held on to some of those destructive emotions today I would yet find it incredibly hard to wear my heart on my sleeve. It is just a knee jerk, ingrained, male reaction that I recognize and own now, and have come to realize that there are times when taking ownership is enough. If I had even the basic understanding of male grief after the tragedy, I might have forced myself to do something that, at that time, would have been unnatural and possibly more harmful than good. A full out "me against me" fight directly after the loss would have been an extremely taxing hit on my stress levels. Thankfully, I remained back from the brink as I rode it out for some time just being who I was born and raised to be, right or wrong. I would come close, though, but snapped back to hope one day when, without conscious thought, I just let it go in relative privacy without the self-perceived shame or indignity I felt others would find in me.

I do hope recounting my journey will help you discover the benefits in releasing your grief in some way, as well. It cannot be repeated enough that so many of those emotions balled into grief are tremendously eroding to your very well-being. I found my place, as you have read, but know your place need not be the shower of which I speak so much. That is where the grief would initially burst from deep inside my spirit, and where I frequently seek that wonderful emotional release even today. Your shower might instead be your car during a long commute, your workshop on weekends, or even out in the barn while feeding the chickens. As long as it is a regular, solemn place where you can find peace and spend time alone with your memories and grief, it will be perfect. I actually have a backup to my showery haven in a spare room I converted into a gym, complete with a weight bench, treadmill and of course a loud stereo system for my workout music. Still to this day, I fire up my favorite playlist of songs, which either motivate me to workout harder or purposely allow me to remember Jonathan. In the music and the workout routines, I can be lost in inspiration or lost in grief, depending on what plays at the moment. I sing along loudly and joyfully with the uplifting refrains when I take my thirty-second rest between sets of bench presses, leg lifts or whatever. Then, when a song plays that brings me to tearful thoughts of my son, I sing my sadness, anger, sorrow, and guilt along with the artist. It is an amazing and wonderful release of emotions. By the way, the dirty secret, at least for me, is being an incredibly tone deaf singer. No matter what noises escape the room and find the unlucky ears of others, whether singing or wailing along, it all sounds like cats fighting at midnight and no one is the wiser. The point being, though, I found a way to get my emotions out and stop the dirty, nasty ones from chewing me up inside.

Absolutely one of the healthiest things I did for my well-being was to gain a fundamental understanding of why it is predominantly a male tendency to hold in the many emotions that surround grief. Looking back, I now know that once I got to the point where I allowed the pain to flow I began the first step to what will be a life-long journey to seek self-awareness, spirituality and a new relationship with my creator. Additionally, one of the driving forces behind this publication was to respect and honor the wonderful legacy that my son left behind for me by allowing my experiences to help others. The research and findings by medical personnel of Jonathan's defective heart helped so many other unfortunate children that he never actually got a chance to meet. Therefore, if reading of my journey helps even one grieving father, than I have served well. It is my hopes that in doing so I can add to a void which exists on the bookshelf topic of fathers who have lost a child.

While certainly not all men fall under the broad category of the stereotypical male, the majority of us will shun the thought of seeking professional help, as we feel it will show vulnerability and weakness. For many, including myself, we will follow our instinctive wirings and read a book or two, but only if we must. Admittedly I am of the "if all else fails, read the instruction" mentality, so written materials are usually only considered after I have managed to really screw something up or just cannot figure it out in my head. Unless I am attempting to assemble lawn furniture or disarm a bomb, I believe I will do just fine without help. After all, are directions not just someone else's opinion? And, just where would I get such a temperament, one might ask? Well, from my father of course. In my mind, my loving father was the greatest automotive mechanic in the world, yet I rarely asked his advice for my own car problems. My father, Don Kelly, was a wise man, though, and

I know he purposely programmed me that way early in life. Three of his five kids were boys and in order to maintain peace on his earth, being a personal mechanic to each of his sons was not in his plans. Regardless, I recall how happy I was when I neared the magic age of sixteen and a driver's license, and even happier still when my father surprisingly announced that he would give me a car. It was an old, mid-sixties Dodge that did not run, but I cared not. It was a car! The beater originally belonged to a customer of my father's service station and had broken down on the highway a few days earlier. After the cost of the tow and estimate for repairs, the owner decided it was too much money and signed the title over to my father so he could use it for parts or whatever. Well, "whatever" was his loss and my gain, right?

Nothing is free, however, and the caveat from my father would be that I could have the car but I had to make it run. When he told me that, I held back my desire to squeal like a schoolgirl and managed instead to ask him what was wrong with the car. In lieu of an answer, however, I got only the dad look, which is probably all too familiar to most. If not, picture my father standing in the front doorway of his gas station, his face cast downward as he scrutinized the customer repair ticket in his hands. While he never raised his face, his eyes slowly lifted after my query, however, and gave me that familiar "over the top of the reading glasses" look that told me instantly I was not about to get advice, but paternal life lessons instead. No teenager wants life lessons. Although only seconds, it seemed hours before he finally spoke, "I said if you can make it run, you can have it." I detected a slightly mischievous tone to his voice, and just knew he would chuckle to himself quietly once he turned to walk inside. I got the picture though, and went on to piddle and poke at the car's engine for the next few weeks as I met with failure time and time again. Eventually, and somewhat inevitably, I hung my head low and approached dad for help, almost childlike in the need to tug on his shirtsleeve. Of course, "no" was his quick response and I had to hear another rendition of how I was the son of a mechanic and should be able to fix my own cars. I honestly expected no different when I posed the question, but I was stuck and had to try, at least.

In those days I was pretty much relegated to the front of my father's service station, where along with pumping gas in customer's cars, I would change oil and tires in the front three service bays. Around back, however, were eight more repair bays and a number of professional mechanics my father employed, all of whom were summarily warned not to come to my aide. I would get desperate, though, as sixteen and my license drew near, and one Saturday afternoon ventured back when my father had left the station for home. I approached Donnie, his head mechanic, and acted as if I knew no better when I verbally rolled out my problems before he could dare stop me. He listened patiently though, and when I was through speaking, slyly replied that it sounded like a very tricky problem to him. His advice was for me to go over to the bench and look it up in the repair manual for my car. Repair manual? I never knew such things existed, and that day the clouds parted as I learned of the marvelous secrets my father's mechanics had at their very fingertips. They possessed marvelous, wondrous, and blessed manuals that explained and illustrated even the smallest detail of repair on all sorts of automobiles, including my new, old jalopy. Just how cool was that? Okay, so I make it out to be more than it was, of course, since most gas stations, garages and mechanics had these manuals back then. I just did not know it at the time. The numbers of cars and their manufacturers have grown immensely to date and the data is now accessed on shop computers that contain massive archives for repairs on every make, model, and year for anything with an engine in it. With the complexity of the computer-based cars today, someone turning a wrench could not make a living without this electronic repository. Of course, back when I was trying to make my little junker run, the cars in the United States were predominantly American made and it was extremely rare to see any of these seasoned grease monkeys revert to a repair manual for help. Heaven forbid an experienced mechanic turn to "The Book," because if he did, the cost would be laughter and ridicule from his coworkers. Me? I did not care. I was a teen boy who needed a car, dammit, and delighted to have those empowering books to see me through to my goal. I had skin in the game. My teenage dating life depended on those glorious works of automotive fix-it knowledge. Believe me, soon enough my "beater" ran well enough to support my pre-adult needs.

If I could fast forward from my teen years to just after the loss of my son, I knew from the first moment there would be recommendations of emotional and psychological support to get through the pain any of us would have. Within just the first few sentences from the mouth of my own church pastor there were offers to provide counsel or even direct me towards counseling elsewhere once the funeral services were completed. Yet, I knew in the deep, dark knowledge of "me" there would be no way I was going to engage my ego-fed mind in allowing anyone to know how badly I was doing inside. I might, however, read a book, or mental repair manual, but only if I were really convinced of the need. Sadly, my biggest obstacle for some time after the loss was the conviction that if I kept my emotional grief tucked deeply inside, it could do me no harm. It had worked up to that point and I felt people would think less of me if I showed or talked of my pain openly. Thankfully, I was blessed to have some very kind and concerned friends who frequently suggested I talk with someone about the loss of my son. When I would ask why, the answer, no matter how wise, always just sounded to me like it was just the expected and standard thing to do. If you experience something of the magnitude of losing a child, you just need to talk to someone, no questions asked. It reminded me of my cop days and being sent to the department shrink each time I was involved in a particularly violent event. Protocol after the fact mandated a visit to the department shrink to get your head checked before you could return to duty. Nonetheless, when it became obvious to my caring friends that I would not be lying on anyone's couch and talking of my loss, their suggestions changed to the thought I should at least find a book or two on grieving. As the suggestions continued to come, I finally resolved myself to the possibility I might be messed up for actually feeling okay.

Was I supposed to be on the verge of lunacy, and because I was not, something was actually wrong with me? Maybe I would read a "manual" or two after all, but just out of idle curiosity and the ability to tell my friends I had done so.

I am sure I would have read enthusiastically too, if only the books were available on the retail market. A great many do focus on grief after the loss of a child, as well as the loss of a parent, dog, or even a houseplant. Unfortunately, all the readily available books seemed to be targeted towards the grieving wife or mother, or the grieving child who sadly lost a parent, sibling, or playmate. We are absolutely blessed that there are such abundant publications available, but the same resources for men are almost non-existent. Nevertheless, I was willing to read and turned to a woman and good friend who I have remained in contact with since our days together in high school. Since then that incredibly intelligent lady had homeschooled her four children, all of whom went on to graduate from major universities. Two have attained Master's Degrees while the other two are currently following suit. I reasoned that if learning material was what I was after, regardless the topic, this self-reliant, homebound librarian and curriculum mole could very well be the best search tool available. She enthusiastically accepted the challenge and went to work, but within only a few short days despondently informed me she had found very little. She was not empty handed, however, as she actually located one book focused specifically on the grieving father. After reading the reviews, she actually took the time to download and read the eBook version herself before having a printed copy delivered directly to me. Of course, I gratefully, willfully, and openly read the book cover to cover and when complete, reported it had been of great help. In fact, it was to some extent, but I admit now to being more obliged to my friend's efforts than honest about my opinion.

The book was very well written and had great content, but eventually focused solely on an opinionated mandate that grieving fathers must seek counseling in order to move towards healing. While I absolutely do not begrudge the author's suggestions for peer group or professional intervention, my ego was just not going to allow that. Right or wrong, I had reasoned that if I could actually seek professional help I would not have looked for that book in the first place. That was my take, anyway, and mileage may vary for others. Regardless, the point is that for now there exists a large void in self-help literature for grieving men in general and more specifically, the grieving father. The lack of publications for men who experienced any loss at first seemed a little odd to me, as if maybe I was just looking in the wrong places. It would become more logical to me later, though, as I decided to look for and read other books and research publications that dealt specifically with emotions and the way they are not only processed by males versus females, but expressed as well. I would soon become somewhat fanatical in the topic, fueled largely by the fact I was learning so much about my own personal development and idiosyncrasies. While it excuses little, I found a scapegoat in the well-documented fact that the majority of men and women are hardwired to be who we are from the moment of conception. Speaking only for the men here, we are not only programmed in the womb, but also through our environment after birth, growing up with such advice as "Be a man", "Toughen up", and "Only little girls cry."

There was a time when no amount of study or published book on grief would have helped move me towards healing, though. After the loss of Jonathan I purposely tucked away an enormous amount of anguish and kept it bottled up inside so others would not think me unmanly. Certainly, tears flowed from my eyes as my brother read the eulogy aloud at Jonathan's funeral services. I had written those words and knew I could not recite them without exposing myself to all. I was also teary eyed as my son's body was interred in his grave, and shamefully admit that I took notice of others in attendance that day and ordered myself not to breakdown in front of them. I did, however, convince myself that had better show at least a few tears, or else people would think I had not loved my son at all. It is difficult to think back and not feel repulsed in myself for considering my own "image" before the heartbreak I felt for my son. How could I consciously measure the amount of sentiment to display so that others would know I was a loving father? I do know now, however, those actions were no indication that I did not love my child. Those self-checks, if you will, were a natural part of me being a man, instinctively responding to the programming I had unknowingly received from both nature and nurturing. The act of openly wailing, begging God, screaming in anger and disbelief, even though I might have wanted to, would have actually been forced and unnatural to who I really was at the time.

What was not natural, however, was that beyond the funeral services for my son Jonathan, I allowed the pre-programmed me to carry on. I had survived, and as badly as it hurt, had to maintain my own life. I had been incredibly functional in front of others because I tucked those feelings down deep inside when they came. If I kept doing so, in my logic, I would always survive and the loss of my child, no matter how tragic, would not change me one bit. It all sounded so good, but in fact I was changing for the worse already, I just did not realize it. Somewhat subconsciously, I removed and or avoided anything which reminded me of Jonathan when I traveled through the house. I learned not to allow myself to focus when I passed by his room or my eyesight fell upon a picture of him on the wall. I would purposely avoid little George, who had been my son's best friend for what seemed like forever. He would frequently call on the phone and ask to come by the house to just talk and be close to Jonathan again. It seems his young mind had a better handle on pain than mine. Yet, I just could not bring myself to let that happen. But, I looked at George and I saw Jonathan. If I talked to George, I thought of Jonathan. Thinking of Jonathan made me well up inside and I would fight hard to keep those feelings from coming out, not only just in front of others any more, but in front of myself as well.

Socially, whether at work or with friends, I wondered if others looked at me with pity, as I was the poor soul who had lost a child. I wondered consciously if they were treating me differently than before and I slowly removed myself from those I wrongly suspected. No one wants to be felt sorry for. Being a rock and stalwart, however, had done me well and if I kept it up, all would be good. Yet, I failed to take into account that those feelings of absolute sorrow, anger, guilt, and loneliness were not magically going to leave my heart simply because I consciously kept them corralled inside. Emotions are extremely powerful and just as instinctive to our very survival as thirst, hunger, and fatigue. While the majority may be temporary in nature, they must be recognized and responded to in some fashion to keep them from becoming permanent and damaging. If pushed back too long they would find a home in that place which serves as our moral compass, the subconscious mind. That is where we experience almost reflex-like responses to life's situations, such as instantly coming to aid of the fallen or being truly grateful for the kind attention of others. Our emotions will find a way to be expressed, and when it comes to the especially destructive ones such as anger and guilt, we do not want them corrupting our inborn sense of right and wrong. We want them under control and responded to before they become a part of who we are.

Monday morning, January 13, was roughly a half year after I lost my son. The hot shower was doing its duty of washing the sleep from my eyes and taking the morning chill off my toes. Thoughts ran freely through my mind, unfiltered and undirected as usual. I was heavily into woodwork as a hobby and although I do not recall specifically, it is a good bet I mentally pondered the purchase of some new shop tool.

Although I did not care to understand my own psyche in those days, I knew I often tricked myself into buying a new tool by mentally picturing a project that would need one that I did not already own. Genius, right? I dangle my own carrots in my mind. My thoughts in the shower that morning eventually turned to the weather. The local news had talked about the possibility of snow overnight, although maybe only an inch or two. That was not much but for anyone who has lived in the Mid-South, an inch or two of snow still wipes out the bread and milk aisles at the local stores in the blink of an eye. Even as adults, the thought of snowfall will elicit a happy sort of anxiety with the prayer that maybe school would be canceled and replaced with sledding, snowball fights and building snowmen.

That morning in the shower, I relished in the childlike anxiety for a few moments before my thoughts wandered towards fatherhood and I impulsively wondered if Jonathan would have school that day. With that thought I froze. Where did that come from? I quietly scolded myself for letting the notion that Jonathan was still in my life creep back into my mind. I had retrained myself on so many areas of loneliness along the way, as well. I no longer thought Jonathan was moving around upstairs in his room whenever I heard the dog jump off his bed. I was over the reflex sensation that each time the back door opened, Jonathan would come bopping through just looking for something to eat. Yet, there he was right back in my drifting mind. The thoughts then caused that familiar knot in my forehead that only comes when tears are building. I immediately went into defense mode and self-initiated the familiar fight to hold the pain inside, but would it be enough? I looked to the wall where the showerhead protruded and pictured Jonathan's bedroom that lay just on the other side of that thin wall. Unconsciously, I lifted both arms, placed my wet palms on the tiles, and watched as the water dripping from my hands left streaks down through the condensation. As the knot welled, I moved the top of my head directly under the shower spray and felt a moment of calm stillness where I thought I held the flood of emotions at bay. Little did I know my emotions had just backed up a bit and taken a running start, as the first attempt at breaking through had failed. Apparently, the emotions knew a little more momentum was required and with the second surge, my grief spewed outwards for the very first time since my child died. I cannot tell you verbatim what the words were. The experience was justifiably the volcanic eruption of measureless remorse and loss where whatever words came forth were merged with the open flow of tears and shower spray. There were forceful tears that came with open mouth bawling and mixed with vile expressions of my hatred towards God. I turned my attention from God to Jonathan and announced loudly to my baby that I was oh, so very sorry. I was not begging for forgiveness. Instead, I exclaimed to my son that I should never be forgiven for not protecting him as I had always promised. For my failure, I did not deserve the grace that might come from forgiveness. I would tell him over and over how very sorry I was, although it made me feel no better.

Amid my deep anguish for the very thought my Jonathan was no longer with me I began to run my fingertips along the wet tiles hoping to somehow touch him. I wanted to feel him. I clinched both fists and for a moment thought I could ram them right through the wall and into his room. Maybe, possibly, his soul still dwelled there and I could somehow grab him back into my life. I did not punch though. Instead, I only padded the sides of my fists against the wall slowly, and barely hard enough to feel that I was putting some level of effort to it. I had no real intentions of breaking down the wall as much as I wanted the symbolism, I suppose now, and the anger somewhat subsided. I then turned my palms back towards the tile and moved in closer, laying both forearms and the side of my face against the wet ceramic, pictured Jonathan sitting on his bed, and sobbed loudly. Soon, the emotional chaos was spent and out of exhaustion, I dropped to my knees as the desire to vocalize the pain and sorrow ebbed away. Then, after a few short minutes of head down thought, I physically and spiritually felt my Jonathan there with me. He was there with me. I am not trying to say I felt Jonathan in the shower with me as much as I felt him inside of my own spirit. He was there in my very heart and soul. I felt his love within me that moment and I smiled upwards with tear filled eyes and simply whispered, "Hi, baby."

I said no more words to my son, as I knew the moment was not about trying to talk but instead an unspoken connection that came as I felt him inside. He brought forth to me a thought of who I had been over the past several months since he passed, and I realized the shame as if he had just breathed that reality into my body. I suddenly knew that nothing I had done since he passed had honored who he was or what he had done for me. I always said that my beautiful, gifted child cheated me out of leaving my legacy to him. Instead, he left his for me. He taught me humility and compassion. He taught me never to give up and that our natural instincts are to survive and be happy. Most of all he taught me how to receive, and surprisingly, how to give unconditional love to others. He was the one person I would have honestly laid down my own life for. For him, this was not something I said with abandon. It was God's truth. His love of life, family and friends had been everything I wanted to grow up to be, but did not even aspire to until he came in to my life. That morning in my shower my son came back into my life and told me I could no longer ignore his love, his memory, or his legacy. My child lovingly admonished me that morning and changed my life yet again. Since that day, I have purposely gone to the shower many times just to join him, feel him, and be with his spirit. I may do that less and less these days as the journey he has set me on has taken me to the undeniable realization that he is with me in heart, spirit, and love always. He is with me every day and everywhere, and watches to see what I do with the examples he paid so dearly to leave behind for my own growth.

I will try with all my heart to not disappoint him.

The Rejection of Guilt

"Nothing but man of all envenomed things, doth work upon itself, with inborn stings."

~John Donne

"Hey, Dad. What's for dinner?" I have heard those words play in my mind so much they will stay with me until I am gone from this world. They were said in a playful way, since Jonathan knew the decision of dinner choice was totally up to him, and asking was just meant as a gentle tease towards his father. We had been through so many pre-surgery nights at our house that it became tradition for me to cook or buy Jonathan's dinner of choice the night before. He actually loved my cooking and I used the little perk of making whatever he wanted the night before as a reward or comfort when he was younger. I tried to feed his anxiety with food, I suppose. Thus, it had become a custom over the years and something I expected when I walked in the door from work. That evening, Jonathan was in his typical teenage spot, splayed out on the living room couch playing video games on widescreen TV. It was just after five o'clock and as I walked through the end of the kitchen that joined with the living room I responded, "I don't know buddy. What do you want?" He said he did not know and would think about it, leaving me not really annoyed, but a bit anxious because I was conscious of the time as well, as the fact I would invariably have to run back up to the grocery store if he wanted something not on hand in the fridge.

There were things that needed to be done to get ready for his surgery. We still had to get his recovery room backpack stocked up with goodies and a change of clothes to come home in, as well as gathering his medications and school books in case he needed them. We had to get to bed early too, since Jonathan had been scheduled for the first surgery of the day at Le Bonheur Children's Hospital in downtown Memphis. That was at least a thirty-five minute drive from the house, and meant we would be on the road at 4:30 in the morning. "Do you want steak?" I asked. "Naw," came his response. Wow, I thought to myself. Steak was his favorite food and he was turning it down. "Pizza," I offered. Another "Naw," from Jonathan. "Okay. Figure it out soon, buddy. We have to get the show on the road." "Hey? How about Chinese, Dad?" I knew right away Jonathan was testing me, but in a playful way. There was no malice. While not more so than steak, he did enjoy Chinese, but he also knew I hated ordering it. In our house, it usually took twenty to thirty minutes for entrée choices to be decided after menus were passed back and forth a dozen times. First choices would be debated and changed for second and sometimes thirds.

Then there would be the whole rice issue, too. Those meals that included white rice had to be exchanged for fried, and those with fried rice had to be exchanged with white. Apparently, it was just some type of conspiracy or oversight by whoever made up the Chinese menu, as the default rice listed with the entrée was never right for anyone in our house. Oh, do not let me forget the soup. Jonathan's mother loves both egg drop and wonton soups. She would never order them as part of the meal, but instead would order a pint of each and enjoy them over the next few days straight from the fridge. Yes, egg rolls were needed too, right? On the other hand, do we want spring rolls instead? Finally, when the chaos of determining what to order was done, I still needed to call the restaurant. In doing so, I would get the pleasure of speaking with the very nice Chinese woman I have spoken to at least a hundred times over the years. She has always been so cheerful, but one would think that after as many conversations as we have had together, one of us would drift closer to understanding the other's dialect. We never did, though.

Regardless, I assume it was possible that some of my distaste for ordering had something to do with my anxiety and poor response when Jonathan asked "Hey? How about Chinese, Dad?" I will never forget the words of my response, ever, as I snapped back, "Hey, come on buddy, it's not your last supper." What did I just say? I stopped still in my tracks across the kitchen while a lightning bolt of shame traveled from my heart to my head. What a horribly inappropriate thing to say. Yet I instantly knew to let it go so not to even raise the thought about such horrible thoughts and the evening went on without anyone calling me on my words. I do not even recall what we ate for dinner that night, however, it would be the last meal I would ever share with my beautiful, loving, and playful child. He would not survive his surgery the following day.

I would carry the guilt for those poorly uttered words with me for a very long time to come. Was I right in feeling that way? For the longest time after the loss, my mind reeled feverishly with the need to find a reason why my son had died, even if it meant it was my fault. So bad was my need for an answer that I actually considered a thoughtless, tasteless comment might have somehow influenced Jonathan or even God in some emotional or ethereal way. Nevertheless, I was certainly not right in feeling that way. My comment did not create any action or lack of action that contributed to his passing, and later when that truth was recognized, I traded my feelings of guilt for those comments in for shame. Shame I could handle, as it serves to make us aware we could do better. Unfounded, false guilt, on the other hand, is absolutely one of the most self-destructive emotions we can experience. So many of the other emotions that come bundled into grief are strong on their own, but guilt can be the real trickster in the mix. Early on, guilt may not manifest itself as strongly as other negative emotions, but it is there waiting to leap into action at its first chance. For me, it took an early backseat to anger and sadness, and it would not be until they both eased just a bit before guilt stepped in to fill the space left behind. Everything I did before and during the events that led up to Jonathan's death became suspect in my mind as guilt crept up on each of them. Later, as I began down a path towards healing, I would look back and recall the deep, anguishing feelings I suffered when I was convinced I might have contributed to his death. While false guilt tried to disguise itself as an answer to why such a tragedy took place, it really just trapped me in a place where other areas of healing were ignored.

I would like to spend a brief moment for the summation of my amazing son's life, beginning from his arrival in this world. As a newborn, Jonathan was brought into life with only half of a heart and diagnosed with the congenital heart defect known as Hypo-plastic Left Heart Syndrome. The left side of his heart had failed to develop in the womb and when born, Jonathan stood a good chance of not surviving even a few days of life. However, God would intervene on his behalf and brought an amazing pediatric cardiothoracic surgeon into our lives. Before the tender age of only two and a half, Jonathan would undergo three separate open-heart surgeries, each a part of the overall rebuild of his precious heart. The procedure had to be done in three stages, as his young body would not physically be able to tolerate the entire procedure at once. While Jonathan lay in recovery after the third and final open-heart procedure, with family huddled lovingly around his little hospital crib, I quietly, privately celebrated the news that the procedure had gone very well. Even with the great news, I was not lost to the heartbreak I felt for that innocent child who lay in a medical coma and wrapped in miles of tubes, wires, and tape that covered almost every part of his tiny body. I was also not lost on his will to survive, either, having overcome so much in his few short years. After each of those three life-saving operations, there was normally a very brief appearance by Jonathan's remarkable surgeon, who would say a few words of encouragement and then quickly walk off into the unseen sunset in my mind. All of the follow up talk would be handled by Shelly, the surgeon's Physician's Assistant, or PA for short. Shelly was pleasant, down to earth and one of us. She doted over Jonathan and played an integral role in his survival, so to me she was family. We talked around the recovery crib, which resembled an elevated metal cage on wheels, while the constant sound of blip, beep, blip from the vital stats monitors droned in the background. Nervous anxiety filled my questions and Shelly's responses slowly brought on levels of ease that I dearly needed to have. Before long, the conversations were light and at times not even focused on Jonathan. Then, after a bit of silence when we were just looking down at Jonathan, searching for an area of bare skin to stroke with a loving, comforting finger, Shelly casually mentioned something that could have easily been discounted as small talk. Yet, the casualness did not get by me as she said, "By the way, Doctor Akl has decided that Jonathan will need another surgery to put in a pacemaker. The surgeries have caused so much scar tissue on his little heart it won't be able to beat properly on its own."

Pacemaker? You have to be kidding me. Jonathan had already done the improbable. He had not only made it beyond his first two days of life, he had survived three open-heart surgeries and miraculously bounced back from each miraculously well. Yet after all that we were told that this poor, innocent child would have to undergo yet another surgery to implant a pacemaker in his body, which he would need for the rest of his life. After several day's wait following the last open-heart procedure, his surgeon returned and assaulted my child's body once again. After many, many nerve-wracking hours, the procedure was successfully completed. Because the doctor had a few minutes before his next appointment, I had the opportunity to sit and talk with the man who had given life back to my child. He talked about the heart condition for a few moments as if I was a rookie to all of it. I wanted to tell him just how learned I had become on the condition and the procedures he had done, but knew I would have still just seemed an idiot at his level. It was best if I just listened until I had the chance for questions. When the opportunity came, the most important question I had was one you could probably guess, "What's next for Jonathan?" His answer was quick, without much compassion, and very to the point. However, it was also very sweet to hear when he said, "We'll take a look at him when he is eleven or twelve and see how he is doing. If we need to do some more work, we will." He said this at the same time he stood and began to walk out of the small, private consult room where we spoke. It was a good thing he was a busy man, and one of few words. Had the good doctor remained he would have been witness to almost three long years of anxiety as it departed my body and as I sat back down, I became as limp as a wet towel on a poolside lounge chair.

For his part, the surgeon was correct. There would be no further surgeries for Jonathan on the procedure that gave him a functional two-chamber heart. The Pacemaker became an issue though. Jonathan burned through a pacemaker battery almost yearly, which was initially chalked up to him being a very active little boy. When Jonathan was around the age of six, his pediatric doctors discovered the quick drain on the pacer was due to a defective lead that traveled from the battery to the heart. One of the two leads, which carried the impulses to beat, was bad and retarded the flow of energy, causing the battery to push harder to send the signal to the heart. Because a new lead would necessitate another open-heart surgery, we decided to stick with swapping out pacers as frequently as needed, since that was far less invasive to his body. Around the age of twelve, however, his pediatric cardiologist had enough and the open-heart was performed to replace the defective wire. For the first time since he received a pacemaker, the battery life readout showed that it would be ten years or more before a replacement would be needed. I remember that I joked with Jonathan that he could drive himself for his next pacer change, although he obviously found no humor in that at all. In his mind and heart, nothing would ever be done to him without his dad by his side. Along with the pacemaker changes over the years, Jonathan also went through a number of heart catheterizations for the sole purpose of sticking a camera up in the heart just to see how things were going. Although it sounds simple enough, each still required Jonathan to be sedated, and put on life support and go through a few weeks of inactivity while the incision to his artery healed.

If all of his heart procedures were not enough, around the age of eight or so, my little buddy developed chronic sinus issues and severe sleep apnea. The resolution would be a very painful removal of his tonsils and adenoids. As silly as it sounds, I was almost happy to have my son going through a surgery that any child might have to endure. I, however, did not earn any trust points with my son when before the operation I assured him I felt no pain at all when I had my tonsils removed as a child. I adamantly guaranteed he would be in and out of the hospital in no time and spend a few wonderful days out of school frolicking in front of the TV and his video games. I was so off base, it was pathetic. He spent what seemed like weeks in painful agony on the couch while giving me the big, hairy eyeball each time I neared. I lost a little "street cred" with my boy that day. Over the short sixteen and half years of Jonathan's life, he would undergo surgeries in numbers I am not ashamed to admit I cannot count. Dozens? Yeah, probably. Maybe more. Forgive me, they just all meld together in my mind now. I cannot even tell you how many pacemaker changes he went through, but I can tell you that every procedure was dangerous for his condition. After each, though, Jonathan recovered amazingly quick, stunned his doctors, and earned quick releases from days' worth of hospital stays. Surgery and recovery became a way of life for our household. Normally we would pack an overnight backpack and head off for the hospital around four or five in the morning. The small talk in the car would center on his need to show the doctors in the recovery room that he could eat and pee by the end of the day. Usually, if he could accomplish those little milestones, they would let him go home. Not to badmouth any hospital, but the longer a recovering patient sticks around, the greater the chance of picking up a virus or something else bad. Hospitals are just packed full with sick people, you know, so I encouraged Jonathan's bodily functions often during recovery.

Around the age of twelve, Jonathan's rebuilt heart started to take a bit of a turn for the worse. His oxygen saturation began to drop over time and it was discovered his heart was actually growing collateral veins, or what I called cheater veins. Due to the pressure inside, his heart tried to relieve that pressure by actually growing veins that allowed his blood flow to bypass his lungs. Normally, the blood would have picked up oxygen there before being brought to the heart and pumped to the

SOMETIMES I CRY IN THE SHOWER

body. The cheaters skipped the lungs altogether and dumped oxygen free blood into Jonathan's heart and therefore oxygen free blood to every cell of his body. Call me odd, but when I learned of this condition I could not help but be amazed in the body's ability to adjust, although in this case it was actually harming itself further. The relief for this condition was for Jonathan to undergo a catheterization through the femoral artery in the leg where coils were placed around the cheaters. Those coils would then choke off the blood that flowed through the cheaters and allow only oxygen rich blood from the lungs to be dumped into the heart.

Further, one of the difficulties with the heart rebuilt at such a young age would become apparent as Jonathan's body began to reach adult size. As part of the overall heart reconstruction, Jonathan's main artery had been surgically reattached at the heart. As he aged, the artery would not grow along with the rest of the heart and its small size was restricting the full flow of blood. Thus, his doctors had decided that while inside during the cath, Jonathan would also receive a stint to the artery to open flow and further decrease the pressure. All went well and Jonathan flourished for a couple years before his oxygen began to drop again, and at the age of fourteen, another heart cath was performed and cheaters coiled. Once again, Jonathan's oxygen level spiked for some time and life would go on as normal for a few years as my handsome boy went from Junior High to High School, became a budding golf phenom, as well as a daily host to a yard and house full of friends. At sixteen, however, his regular cardiac checkup revealed his oxygen levels had once again dropped and it was time for another roundup of the cheaters. The fateful surgery that would end with his precious heart failing in the recovery room afterwards was just another "routine" cath to both band up new cheater veins and look around the heart at possible long-term solutions to stop them from forming. Much like the frequent pacemaker changes, the cheater banding had become something that was just a necessity to maintain his oxygen levels, and if it kept him alive forever, I accepted that they would be done whenever needed.

When we checked into the hospital the morning of his procedures, no one, including his surgeons knew how tired Jonathan's little heart was from all the abuse over the years. When the procedure was completed and Jonathan brought to the recovery room still unconscious but alive, I sat with his surgeon and discussed future options, which included continued banding, as well as the possibility of a heart transplant. The doctor wanted to hold off on further discussions until after Jonathan recovered, but he had imprinted the thought of a heart transplant in my mind, including all the cautions and possible dangers. Cautions aside, I sat back in a chair beside my sleeping child and daydreamed of the life my son would have if he could run at full speed, not have to stop for a rest in the middle of a driveway basketball game, and even walk an entire eighteen holes of golf. What an amazing life my child could experience if the handicaps of the past sixteen and a half years were suddenly erased? Jonathan would not come out of his anesthesia after that fateful surgery though, and as efforts through the night to revive him failed, his heart finally stopped beating just as the sun rose the next morning. He moved on to a place where he would do all of those things without the need for a new heart and he could play thirty-six holes of golf if he so desired.

After he passed and guilt started to become a predominant thought in my mind, it came on hard. I felt guilt for so very much I did or did not do, including even letting the surgery happen. I had cancelled surgeries before in the past because they did not feel right. In one case just about a year and a half prior I simply walked out of pre-op with Jonathan and told the attending nurse to have someone call us about rescheduling. There are people still to this day who say they cannot believe I actually did that. I was not obnoxious about it. It just did not feel right when we arrived that day at five in the morning. Jonathan had been scheduled for the first surgery that day, but we were told that the surgeons had to take an emergency case into Jonathan's assigned operating room, so there would be a delay. I certainly understood that. However, by around ten in the morning we were advised again that the surgeons had to take a second emergency case in and Jonathan's procedure would be delayed a little longer. The nurse left and I looked at my son who had been doing his best to hide his anxiety all morning. I knew, however, as a father that recognized every facial expression that child ever had, he was emotionally tapped out. Further, I discovered it was Jonathan's surgeon and his team performing those back-to-back emergency procedures and had to wonder just how fresh and alert were they going to be when working on my son. That was enough and my child and I found the pre-op nurse and ignored her pleas to stay when I told her to have the surgeon reschedule. We did reschedule the operation, and it was performed without any issues a month or so later.

Two years later Jonathan and I would again find ourselves at the hospital before sunrise for the heart catheterization that would tragically end with the loss of his life. After we were checked in and were called to pre-op, the nurse coincidentally informed us that Jonathan's doctor was performing an unscheduled emergency surgery and his cath would be delayed for a short but unknown amount of time. This time, I would wait it out with Jonathan, as it seemed to have caused quite a bit of angst among the doctors when we walked out before. This time I would not see him alive the next day. When I lost my child after this delayed start, the guilt would come, as I wondered why I had not taken my child by the hand and walked out again. If I had only done the same that morning as I had in the past, Jonathan would still be with me today, I reasoned. Moreover, after the surgery took place, why did I not do more in the recovery room when it was obvious to me, his father, that something was not right with my child? I knew in the depth of my very soul something was wrong, but we were in the pediatric intensive care unit of Le Bonheur Hospital, one of the preeminent hospitals for child heart care in the country. When the PICU nurse continued to inform me that Jon's slow recovery from the anesthesia was normal and he had seen it many times before, I wanted to scream that I, his father, had not seen it before. As his father, I had been there for every one of Jonathan's previous surgeries and that kid had always exceeded the norm when it came to recovery. He had been through surgeries that were much tougher than a heart cath and had no problems coming around, yet the PICU nurse told me all was just fine. Did I let my guard and my son down?

What would have happened if I had stood in the hallway and screamed for a doctor instead of taking the word of a nurse? I had certainly done it before. Shortly after Jonathan was first born, I took him to a local hospital when he spiked a fever that would eventually go as high as one hundred and eight degrees. When I thought that the young nurse attending my son was satisfied with constantly feeding him a fever reducer that had no effect throughout the evening, I took to the hallway at 3:00am and screamed for a doctor at the top of my lungs. Did my lack of action when I felt something was wrong contribute to losing my child at Le Bonheur? After he passed, I actually went as far as to order a full autopsy on my precious son through an independent hospital and enlisted a team of pediatric cardiologists to review everything. While many thought I was working towards a potential lawsuit, I actually just wanted to know the truth. I had to know. What I would find in the opinions of the review board was that Jonathan's precious heart was just frail and tired. There was no indication that the surgery staff needed to take more precautions up front or that there was malfeasance in the operating or the recovery room. His little heart simply gave out to the point where he would not recover.

I purposely placed this chapter of the book before many because I know, at least for me, guilt was absolutely the most destructive pain I went through after I lost my son. It comes upon us easily after a loss and is one of the most difficult to let pass. Even today, if I am not careful, it can sneak its way back in at any time. Guilt was actually one of the first things I instinctively knew I had to understand when I started my journey towards healing, and obviously had to separate the meaning of true guilt from false guilt. True guilt is the knowledge and evidence that we have purposely done something that brought about a negative effect to others or ourselves. For the most part true guilt can be healthy if it effects a positive change to the character of the person. False guilt is very simply when we only feel an action or inaction resulted in something bad, yet all other signs, including logic, indicate otherwise. In the loss of my child, everything was completely out of my direct control, regardless of any words spoken, actions taken or actions not taken. Sure, I could relive the events before the surgery that lead to his passing and feel guilt for not canceling the procedure, but that would not help. If he did not have the surgery, his health would have eventually deteriorated, and his precious life would have ended over time. I could even go further back and feel guilt for not being more strict on his diet over the years, telling myself he would have been stronger had I not allowed him to sneak candy and cookies from time to time. To this day, if I allow myself, I can find a great many things that could lead to false guilt. However, the critical reality that I had to wrap myself around was that I, in no way, had a single fiber in my being that would purposely allow anything bad happen to my child. When all was said and done, that fundamental fact alone gives me the assurance to let go of guilt.

It is important that I go back and touch on another possible reason why I needed to feel false guilt, as I had only given it a casual mention earlier. As males, we tend to have a natural yearning to explain any catastrophe or tragic event in our lives almost immediately. When all is confusing and things are spinning around, we just want to know the reason why it happened in the first place. False guilt expediently allowed me to find an explanation for the loss, even if it meant I was blaming myself. There had been no expectation things would go wrong with my son. What should have been a simple night in the recovery room ended with Jonathan dying in a place where the doctors and nurses were the best in the business. They surely could not be to blame. Jonathan himself was relatively healthy, besides the low oxygen levels, and had survived far worse surgeries in his past. The answer could not be him, either. What, then, was the wild card that caused his death? I needed someone to be ultimately at fault, and going after myself was simple. That need was so corrosive that it actually led me to believe my shameful comment about his last supper contributed in some way to my son's death. I would find myself ridiculously thinking his passing was God's wrath, karma, a jinx, or whatever.

I have since dealt with my shame for that comment and with what I have discovered along my path to healing, can deal with those false feelings of grief as well. More assuredly, I know Jonathan is within me now, as he has been the whole time. If guilt attempts to find its way back in to my heart, a little angel will just laugh softly and whisper, "No, Dad. No. It wasn't you."

The Programmed Man

*"Feelings are much like waves, we can't stop them
from coming, but we can choose which one to surf."*
~ *Jonatan Martensson*

I sat at my workbench and tried to focus on tinkering. If one can actually focus on tinkering, that was what I was doing. I needed to do something that involved a few minutes of normal. I have come to learn and understand that when the mind, or heart for that matter, experiences a terrible event, trauma, or catastrophe, it will aggressively seek out things that are normal. It wants normal. It needs normal because normal is usually calm and nice. Abnormal invokes fear, and while fear is an emotion we may need to survive, we do not want it hanging around longer than we need it. We do not take fear to parties with us, do we? I wanted normal that morning and I welcomed it like a shot of bourbon. I needed something to do I could control. The male mind is programmed to take control and manage things, and at the time, I had seemed to be in between responsibilities and waiting on others to release their control so I could start controlling again. That was in my very nature, although at the moment not within my immediate ability. Only a few short hours before I sat down at the workbench, my Jonathan had died in my arms, taking away any luxury of a denial stage to trick

36

my mind. I had been there and held that gorgeous boy as his soul returned to our creator.

Of course, for the longest time after he passed I would almost "forget" he was gone and think a noise upstairs was Jonathan bumping around in his bedroom, or when I would see the school bus coming down the road in the late afternoon, think for just a moment it would be stopping at our corner. That morning at the hospital however, I certainly could not benefit from the stage of grief that allowed me to disbelieve he was gone. I managed to get away from the hospital around mid-morning, having tolerated some level of talks with the doctors in attendance when Jonathan's heart gave out during recovery. They were absolutely caring and compassionate to a man who was obviously in shock, but it seemed the common sense questions about what would happen had come and gone, and left them asking such things as did I want a lock of his hair, or did I want a plaster cast imprint of his hand. I recall making the response once, "I have no idea. I am a rookie at this." Of course, no one wants to be a pro, but at the time the response just felt good coming out of my mouth. From the hospital, I seemed to be on autopilot as I instinctively drove straight to my church. I knew it was part of my responsibilities in setting up the services and I felt attached to the church. Jonathan and I were members and on Sundays we would operate the church's sound system together, taking charge of a professional looking mixer board with hundreds of knobs and buttons, many of which we never touched. Even though a weekday, I was grateful the Pastor was in and although he was very consoling, I was just not ready to hear a great deal of "It is God's way" and "Jonathan is with

God now." I wanted to get started on the arrangements but there seemed to be an awful lot of questions about what verse I wanted read, or what hymn should be sung during the service. I will now admit to being a little short with the good Pastor when I answered, "I don't know. I thought that's what I had you for. You're the specialist at this." I got a pained smile and an almost understanding nod from the pastor, as he said he would put together what he thought was fitting and stop by the house later so changes could be made if I liked.

I had nothing to do and a strong desire for normal, yet no place to go but home. Home certainly was not going to be normal. How could it be? Jonathan was not going to be there and that place would never be the same to me again. My workbench where I spent so much of my off time was there, however, and it would be somewhat normal. So, I walked in the side door of the garage, flipped on the TV atop my sawdust-covered refrigerator and sat down on my good ole shop stool to make my hands and mind busy. I recall almost every moment of that morning as if it were today, yet for the life of me cannot tell you what I tinkered with. I say I wanted normal, but I was not going to get it, regardless of my busy, tinkering hands. My mind took over and it could not stay away from that morning in the hospital room. While I was devastated deeply and inconsolably by the loss of my son and the overwhelming shock that came with it, I actually had the shameful thoughts of how I acted in front of the hospital staff. In front of dozens, I begged, encouraged and pleaded with God to spare my child, and then did the same with Jonathan as I begged him to come back to me. That loud, uncontrolled release of pain and disbelief was certainly acceptable and expected for a father who had watched his child pass away. Yet, as I sat at my workbench afterwards I actually made the conscious determination that it had been an embarrassing, unmanly act in front of others, and I surely would not let it happen ever again. That is hard to believe, is it not? While I gave it no thought then, I would begin to recognize and understand the tendency when I began my journey with a simple cry in the shower.

I am certainly not trying to condone the initial disgust for my actions, but I do understand now just how that instinct to hold in emotions which show hurt, pain, and tears of sadness are ingrained in men both environmentally and biologically. Simply put, there is a law of manly emotion almost as real as the law of gravity. Like gravity, you might not see the law of manly emotion, but also like gravity, you will be able to see it in action, and probably do witness it in yourself every day. While I firmly believe neither sex is better than the other, each has traits that make them who they are. Women, in general of course, are empathizers and want to know the emotions of others and openly express their own. Men, once again in general, quite simply do not. There was a skit by a popular comedian who told the story of returning home after work one evening and casually mentioning to his wife that one of the guys at the office was getting a divorce. The wife wanted to know what happened between the unhappy couple with such questions as was one cheating on the other, were there children involved, had they sought out counseling, and many other details. Her husband's only response was that he had no idea, as his buddy had simply mentioned he was getting divorced and when the comedian asked if he was okay, the pal yes. To the comedian, the conversation was over at that point. In the skit, the comedian's wife actually ordered him to call his buddy and hand her the phone so she could get the details. That pretty much sums up a great deal of the differences in the way men and women process feelings.

The skit may also explain why we have limited written resources dealing directly with men and grief. In essence, we are an absent audience, and while I take some liberty with this assumption, who wants to preach to those who will not listen. This became fascinating to me as I began to research the difference in displays of emotions in both men and women separately, and it gave me an interesting glimpse into my own life. One might say it is pretentious of me to think I am no different in many ways from other men. Of course, there are obvious differences in every man. In fact, I have one brother who is several years older than I am and a brother several years younger. While there are certainly some minor similarities in our looks and mannerisms, we are three entirely dissimilar men who grew up in three different social eras. Yet inside, we share the same fundamental tendencies that came from our father and from our genes.

In wanting to understand male versus female emotions, the deeper I looked to gain some level of understanding, the more I found many of my similarities to other men very remarkable. I think part of the journey to healing has been the satisfaction of knowing what I did, while sometimes regretful in retrospect, was something to be expected from a normal "Joe." Keep in mind, I do not say condoned, only expected. Regardless, my research led to the ever-obvious impact that just being born unto the world as a male had on me. This is the environmental affect and it is during this period most males are taught, through both words and deeds, that men do not show emotions perceived as weak or feminine. When the term "Nurture or Nature" is used, the environment is what is referred to by the word nurture. It is during nurturing that we are subjected to lessons like "Toughen up," "Be a man," "Don't be a sissy," and so much more. We are hungry for information as young kids and watch our fathers and role models intently, looking for signs and watching for reactions to life's challenges. As a young boy, I would often look to those older, not so much to gauge their emotions, but more so to measure their physical response to events out of the norm. If a UFO dropped straight out of the sky during a family picnic and touched down in the potato salad, I wanted to look to Dad to see if it was all right to run away, or just act as if everything was going to be all okay. Everyone else would be looking at Dad, too, and he would never have shown fear or anxiety, even if he felt it. He might show anger for the potato salad, maybe, but nothing more.

Side dish humor aside, I can recall being a child and attending a few funerals of my parent's close friends. My mother, as well as most of the women in attendance would cry, of course, while Dad and all the other men were quiet, calm, and respectful. I was rather observant back then, growing up as the middle of five children. Some would call the middle child the "mediator" or the "diplomat." Me? I learned to watch. Again, I was not watching for emotions, per se, but for reactions. For example, at the funeral for a man my folks had been very close friends with, I watched as my mother consoled the daughter of the dearly departed. Mom approached and only looked at the woman and they both instantly broke into tears and melded into what must have been a five-minute embrace. There were sobs and moans with all manner of odd, squeaky noises. Mom asked the young woman if she was going to be okay, to which the woman replied, "I don't know. Can you stay? I could use a friend." Just a few minutes later, on the other hand, I watched as my father approached the son, in his mid-thirties or so, looked him in the eye, shook his hand, and gave his condolences. My father asked the son how he was "making it," and if there was anything he needed. The son simply replied with a kind, "Thank you. I'm good, though." That would be immediately followed by a serious and stoic, "We need to get this thing over with. I've got to get back to the shop." That was just one example of the scenarios of environmental programming that many men of my age were subjected to in our formative years. In fact, I never once saw my father shed a tear until very, very late in his life and only then because my mother had passed away.

As males, we come out of those formative years and slam right into the pimple-infested age where our bodies begin producing testosterone like mountain folk making moonshine. If we have not been exposed already, we are getting involved in more competitive, hard-hitting contact sports where only the most talented and "toughest" make the team. Soon, the magical allure of the opposite sex, and well, sex in general, decides to join the party and all of a sudden, "spin the bottle" doesn't sound like such a bad game after all. The fairer sex was, without question, the top issue on the average boy's mind, supported closely by the need to appear tough and man-like. As we leave our teens and enter the adult world, the necessity for showing manhood and controlled emotions are still a major influence in our development. Whether we enter college, go into military service, or begin our journey in developing a career, we cannot allow emotions to get in the way. I could never imagine making it through Marine Corps Boot Camp as a young recruit at Parris Island, South Carolina if I had not been raised to keep my emotions in check. I am sure my Drill Instructor might have had a difficult time understanding my panic induced tears on the rappelling tower as I leaned back into the rope harness from what felt like a mile high above earth. I had no choice, though. Nor was any given or offered to me. I was going to lean back in the empty air with nothing to support me except a rope strangling my crotch. Was I scared? I was frightened tremendously and wanted my mommy. Was I going to cry? Absolutely not. If I had been five years old at the time, would I have cried? You're damned skippy I would have. At ten, I would have cried, just not at first. You would have to give me about thirty seconds of trying not to, but that would not work and the tears would come. Maybe by the age of fifteen or so I might not cry, but the look on my face would be nothing short of total terror.

As young males, we are generally conditioned through our environment to keep our emotions in check by those who nurture us. While this can certainly come from our mothers, predominantly it is passed down by our fathers, other male role models and often from our peers. I would be the nurturing male attitude influence on my Jonathan, who was submitted to so many medical procedures throughout his short life. While I would like to believe that as a newborn child and then toddler, he had no real concept of the life threatening perils he faced in his back-to-back open-heart procedures. However, that would obviously change as he grew older. His mind gained awareness of life, along with the fear and expected anxiety for each upcoming medical procedure, regardless of how minor. Along the way, I would subconsciously nurture him with encouragements, which included "Don't be afraid. You're a tough boy," and all manner of the typical tough boy words you might expect. These words were meant to be comforting to him, of course, hoping that to hear this from "Daddy" would give him assurance, but right or wrong, it was environmental programming as well. I will also admit that those words I spoke comforted me as well. Yet, I was not without fatherly instinct and compassion for my son when it came to my instinctive and dutiful programming. I had told earlier of a heart cath procedure when Jonathan's scheduled surgery was pushed back twice while his doctors tended to other emergencies. As he and I waited to be taken back into the operating room area, we were notified of the successive delays and regardless of all the reinforcements and encouragements from me, I could see the outer tough shell of this dear child break down over time. I was in a tough spot at that point. I watched that little twelve-year-old steel himself throughout the evening before and the ride to the hospital, as I reassured him along the way. The first delay caused a reset in his anxiety, as if the nerves started from the ground floor again and began to build as we waited and wondered. Another delay would come and I could see the hours of anxiety over the past few day had taken its toll. I would ask several times if he was all right and was he okay with the wait, and he would tell me he was, but he was done, and so was I. He did not want to admit it, but I could feel it. As soon as I took him by the hand and told him we were out of there, all the fear and anxiety blew out of him like air escaping from an untied balloon. We were barely in the car for the trip home when he passed out, slept through the drive, and finished his day with a long nap on the couch. My little man would not show me his fear that morning because of the nurturing I gave him in the past, right or wrong. Just as I programmed my child, my father passed it down to me, his father to him and so on.

Can we, as men, actually de-program ourselves from what our environment has ingrained within us? Even if the answer were yes, it would not be a simple thing to do. In addition to nurturing, nature has played a separate, yet similar role in making us who we are. It seems that while developing innocently in the womb, males are biologically hard-wired with a predisposition to emotions as well. First, men, if you did not know this, we all began as females in the womb. If you doubt this, consider the fact that, like women, we have nipples on our chest that are completely useless to us since we do not breastfeed our young. There has been some debate whether at some point in our past we shared nursing duties with the mother, but it is largely dismissed in scientific communities. Instead, the undisputed fact remains that we were, by default, initially female after conception, with the identical girlish anatomy, including the nipples that develop in both sexes at around the age of four weeks. The male penis and testicles do not begin to develop until the Y chromosome triggers the release of testosterone at around seven weeks. The nipples, although relatively useless for the male, are of no danger to our health and the body just allows them to remain. Interestingly enough, the only male mammals that do not have nipples are rats, mice and stallion horses.

I had promised earlier in the book not to just regurgitate dry and boring material from research papers, and I will do my best to keep that oath here. Believe me, when it comes to dumbing things down, I am all about that, as I have lived my life begging others to do the same for me. At times my low, sloping forehead seems to get in the way and block big words from entering my head, so I need it with a twist of "regular" speak. Regardless, we all know about testosterone. It is actually the presence of testosterone that creates the male anatomy, and the very lack of testosterone that allows the female to continue in her default mode. The testosterone also breaks down into a chemical called estradiol that will cross into the male brain and create not only minor structural differences, but also the emotional pre-wiring that will greatly influence how men might approach life. Studies of this are often referred to as "Brain Sex," which concludes that through evolution, males are generally wired to be "Systemizers," while females are wired to be "Empathizers." The life of early man demanded strength, strategy, and rules to not only hunt and gather, but to accomplish one of our primal urges of reproduction as well. Therefore, stoicism became the lifestyle where hierarchy, competition, and dominance evolved into the required male attributes. Females had to compete as well, sometimes for that dangerous but instinctive urge to mate, but falling in love and sweet courtships were not all the rage then. Males with the urge to mate were fairly, uh, assertive, and evidence shows that females had to group together frequently to protect themselves and the children from aggressive males. Thus, the primary role of the female became social support, protection, and care of the young. The female brain evolved to maintain social harmony, which meant expressing empathy and constantly surveying the well-being of others around her. A Female needed to do this just to survive, just as men, hunting in the wilds, evolved throughout time with more indifferent, quiet tendencies.

Studies of children in modern times show obvious evidence of these traits quickly after birth. As toddlers, baby girls begin making eye contact much sooner than males and their instinct to study faces increases over 400% just in the first three months of life. Boys? Well, not so much. It seems during all these studies we boys were much more prone to explore our surroundings and not worry so much about what others might be thinking. Interesting research reveals that the female's natural talent for responding to facial gestures is a learned response to caring for newborn children who cannot speak for themselves at birth. Women use their natural abilities to simply look into the baby's face and know what is needed or wanted. There are other obvious differences we simply do not need pointed out to us by researchers, as well. We are all witness to the tendency for little boys to lean towards toy cars, roughhousing and competitive sports, while girls lean towards dolls, social gatherings and more emotional interactions with friends and family. Yes, of course, there are variations to the above and I paint with a broad brush, since we all know male and female friends who do not quite fit into either stereotypical gender mold. As a collective, however, the vast majority of us are somewhat controlled by that little sperm that broke through the egg and caused the spark of a new life. Did that little swimmer bring with it an X or a Y chromosome? It seems we fathers get very little plausible deniability when it comes to the programming of our sons. We sent over the Y chromosome that dumped all the testosterone in the first place, so maybe, just maybe mothers are off the hook for our male response to emotions.

Broad brush aside, one must question whether if we so chose, can we permanently override our inherited and learned programming? We absolutely can, with a concerted effort and only if we genuinely feel it has a negative impact in the desired direction of our lives. Even then, nature is going to be even harder to overcome than nurture. Case in point, I was subjected to the most intensive attempts to strip away all of my pre-programming when I submitted myself to thirteen weeks of Boot Camp hell in the swamps of South Carolina. To make it even more interesting, I chose to go during the sweltering heat of July and August. I can attest that the only thing that equaled the physical trials I was subjected to would be the mental reshaping I was given. I have heard a lot of people voice disgust for what has been called the brutal intensity of Marine Corps Boot Camp and while I was actually there, I might have agreed with them. After I graduated, however, I understood and agreed with the methods and the madness. Regardless of what anyone thinks about our military, no one at any rank wants the men or women they serve with to die in combat. We no longer fight like the Red Coats in the Revolutionary War where men are lined up row after unending row and marched straight towards the enemy's fire. Those front rows were acceptable sacrifices so that the remaining mass of troops could overtake the enemy. Military strategy is now based on defeating the enemy and bringing our troops home alive. To accomplish this there are leaders and there are followers in the military, and while I might be oversimplifying things, when any follower fails to instantly respond to the orders of the leader, troops or soldiers could die. When we as humans are told to go into any situation where the brain perceives a danger, we have an expected and natural propensity to stop and ask why first. It is self-preservation to know the answer, since maybe our brain will actually tell us that rushing into danger is not really such a great idea. Yet, in combat, the delay is not a good thing. A good troop or soldier must trust his or her leader and not question orders when given. Therefore, Marine Corps Boot Camp is specifically intended to strip away the instinct to self-rationalize and have unquestionable and immediate response to all orders.

During the day-to-day duties of being in the service there were many orders to be followed, and as my military programming dictated, I responded to each immediately and without question. Do not get me wrong, many orders to be expected in war were explained in advance during training, but these all became "environmental" and caused my immediate and instinctive response. While I will not use examples of combat training, I can get the point across with examples of some distinguished traditions, or mannerisms, instilled in me during my four years. A Marine never carries an umbrella unless holding one over the head of a lady. To this day, I cannot even bring myself to put an umbrella in my golf bag. My service was back in the mid-eighties, and during my time, a Marine was forbidden from being off the base in a plain, white tee shirt. Today, I will not leave the house in one since plain t-shirts without logos, words, or emblems are meant to be undergarments. Walking around in public in one would be no different that doing so in just my boxer briefs. Back then, I was also taught that a Marine did not keep his hands in pants pockets, as pockets were meant only to carry other objects into combat. As you can guess by now, I never place and keep my hands in my pockets still today. While I have purposely retained those and many other fine traditions programmed in me, I do so only because they are positive and honor my service to the Corps. In the civilian world, however, I had to evaluate the value of charging into actions at work and home based on the words or demands of others. On one hand, I needed to continue those traits while a police officer. Yet, at home and especially later, when I entered private business, I had to reevaluate where the whole idea of unquestionably responding to orders had value for me. It was not easy, since this was an incredibly powerful, core concept intensely drilled into in boot camp and four years of honorable service. As a civilian, however, I no longer faced the potential for combat and the overall trait proved unproductive and in some cases, negative to my life. Would I be able to drop the overall concept of blindly following orders? Yes, I would, and did, but it took a very long time and only after I realized which traits negatively influenced my life. Would I deprogram myself of the umbrella, tee shirt, and hands out of pockets behaviors? No way. Like nipples on the male fetus, they do me no harm.

The natural instincts that came to us in the womb will be far more difficult to alter or overcome, if we even desire to do so. The traits to hold in our emotions are essentially encoded within our very DNA, which means they stand ready to be passed along to the next generation of males, as well. After all, did we not get those qualities from our fathers, who got them from their fathers and so on? Yet, if science tells us we have certain traits because of evolutionary development, it also means we did not have them at the dawn of man. We took them on because they were a positive in our lives at the time, deemed necessary for survival and procreation. By the same logical thought, then, we can devolve those we now recognize as negative in our modern lives. Therein lies the issue of first recognizing our traits and then evaluating which of those are positive, harmless, or negative to who we want to be. Once the negatives are identified, a dedicated and concerted effort must be made to work towards the desired change. I say work towards, since the process will not be a light switch that can be turned on and off at a simple whim. I am working towards devolving the negatives myself, but I am not going to look back and beat myself up over my compulsion to hide my grief. I actually am more disheartened that I held the pain of my loss from myself, convinced if I ignored it, I would always be okay. In doing so, however, I dishonored my son's life memory and delayed the start of my healing. I continue to support anyone who can seek professional counseling, and urge those "devolved" and liberated sons of our fathers to do so. If you are truly like me, however, at least find your shower and privately release those harmful emotions that are bottled up inside of your spirit. I hope that as you read of my journeys in this book, you realize there is still so much of your awe-inspiring life to experience and celebrate.

The River of Grief

"There is no pain so great as the memory of joy in present grief."
                                                    ~Aeschylus

It was early Saturday morning, March 22nd, 2003 and I was doing at least ninety miles an hour west bound on Interstate 66, headed from the outskirts of Washington, DC to just outside the little town of Luray, Virginia. I was not worried about exceeding the speed limit because I had a badge. Actually, I had a badge and federal agent credentials, or creds if you want to say it cool, issued by the US State Department's Bureau of Diplomatic Security. I had taken a private contract position with them immediately after the tragic events of September 11, 2001, and then became deputized through the US Marshals Service so I had jurisdiction regardless of where I traveled. Technically, or legally I should say, I was only authorized to use my creds while I was working in an official capacity for the government. With what was going through my mind, however, I would take advantage of it and "badge" any cop that dared stop me for speeding. To be honest, I was not really worried about being pulled over at all. I was more concerned that I had just spoken to my boss and could not manage to tell him my mother had passed away without breaking down like a baby. I was not breaking down badly, mind you, but the lip quivering, altered voice kind of breaking down. There I was just trying to explain I would not be in for the next several days and the instant the words "my mom died" formulated in my mind, my mouth was no longer under my control. I am not sure I ever got the words out, actually. Before making that call, however, I had done well that morning. I had preserved my manhood and had not broken down once. Yet, all of a sudden, I simply could not tell my boss that my mother had just passed away and I would not be into work for a while. What changed in my armor?

It was probably somewhere around 5:30 or so when the phone rang. I remember thinking that no phone call at that time was going to be a good one. When I answered, I heard the voice of my brother-in-law, Fernando, on the other end. Fernando may be my brother-in-law but he has been in my family since I was thirteen or fourteen years old when he began dating and then married my big sister Debbie. To me, he could not be more family if we shared the same blood but I could count the number of times he and I had spoken over the phone on one hand. Maybe even one finger. That went through my mind and I just knew something was not right. In a millisecond, my mind mixed that thought with the tone in his voice as he spoke, which just oozed with sympathy. "Ronnie, uh, hey, listen…," Then there was that half-second pause we all take when delivering bad news. Yep, something was wrong. What was it? Had something happened to Debbie? God, not one of their five kids, please. However, Fernando would not be calling me to tell me about one of his kids. I would be the last thing on his mind.

My thoughts were spinning like a record on a turntable creating all kinds of bad scenarios in just that split second of time before I heard him continue to speak. I thought to myself, get ready. Here it comes, and he continued, "I'm sorry. I need to let you know your mom passed away late last night and everyone is headed up there to the house," he finished quietly, and with a little hint of duty. As you could imagine my sister was a wreck and could not make any calls, so Ferd stepped in and took the job. He briefly explained that late the night before while sitting on the couch and watching television with my father, mom complained of being cold. She asked my father to get her a blanket from the bedroom and by the time he returned, my mother was unresponsive. She was taken to the hospital by ambulance and never recovered consciousness. I asked about my sister, of course, and when Fernando told me she was upset but all right, I told him I would be on my way and would see them as soon as I got there. Got there? I actually had an overwhelming urge to just crawl back into the bed under the safe world of the covers where I could go to sleep and nothing would be real. I could not, however, as I would be expected at my parent's house. That was the thing to do and I knew it. It was important to do what I was supposed to do and falling apart or dodging reality was not on the checklist. First things first. I had to get out of the house.

My son Jonathan was just a toddler and asleep, as was his mother. I did not really want to wake her because I just knew when I told her she would cry, of course, and there would be tears and questions I had no answers to yet. I also knew she would ask me if I was okay. Of course I was okay. I was always okay, right? It was my responsibility, however, to wake up the wife and let her know what was going on and I did exactly that. As dryly as if I were talking about some distant friend's mother, without a waver or tremor in my voice I calmly explained that Fernando had called to let me know my mother had died unexpectedly. My wife went through the progressions I expected and then offered to get up, get herself and Jonathan ready to go with me, but I told her I needed to get to the family as soon as possible and I would check in with her later. Actually, I knew in my mind that during the time it took for her and my son to get ready I would have a lot of time to not be doing what I thought I should be doing, which was getting to my father, brothers and sisters. My duty right that minute was to get to them because they would need me. They had to need me, because if not, all I would have to think about was the pain and sorrow of losing my mother. With family needing me, I had duties and there was no time for emotions or tears.

My one overwhelming need was to get to family, which meant at least an hour's drive in the car. What a beautiful drive it had always been, too. Interstate 66 was the main road I had to travel and as it left the suburbs of DC, the roadway opened up to the foothills of the Blue Ridge Mountains. Once off the interstate, the drive goes through the old town of Front Royal, Virginia and continues down scenic Route 340 to Luray, where my Mom and Dad lived. They had dumped the suburbs of DC twenty-five years earlier and bought a little country store in Rileyville, Virginia, just a few miles outside of Luray, naming it Kelly's Point Grocery. It was a typical country store, selling a myriad of just about anything inside from fishing bait to food to souvenirs. There was also a two bay garage where my father would do light automotive repairs for customers, but only if he liked them and if he was in the mood. He never charged for labor, only for the cost of whatever part might be needed. Behind the store was a picturesque dirt road made up mostly of red clay, which meandered on about a half mile where it ended in the South Fork of the Shenandoah River, full of trout and small mouth bass. This had been their way of returning to the mountains without getting too far from their kids, grandkids, and even great grandkids. My mom absolutely loved it there and I was making the drive early on a Saturday morning in March, as I had done so many times over the years, wanting so very badly to deny she had passed away. I had been in the car for just a few short minutes, leaving behind the concrete and buildings and had the mountains in sight. I had been taking care of my responsibilities as a son. I received the call and responded that I would be right there with family where I should be. I had informed my wife, showered and responsibly gotten in the car to do what I had to do, and now I was on my way. What was my next check box? What did I have to do next? Well, there was not much I could do in the car but get to where I was going…and think.

My mind would not immediately grasp the fact that my mother was gone and began spinning like a carnival tilt-a-whirl. She just could not be gone. There was no early warning to this and it simply just could not be so. God, not my mother, please. She was the one person in life at the time I thought loved me unconditionally. I could have turned out to be a career criminal or a serial killer, and she would have just smiled and said no one understood me as she does. I was her good boy. There was no way my mother was gone. I just knew I would get to my Mom and Dad's house to find that somehow the doctors had been mistaken earlier and she was recovering peacefully at the hospital. I would just get back in the car and go to her there. The other half of my brain jumped into the fray and told me it was true. It told me I had lost my mother and I had to deal with it. I had to deal with it and I needed something to do, some check box to mark off or I might lose it. I could not make any plans yet, really, as they were not mine to make. That would be my father's job so I would get to him and surely he would give me marching orders and I could take care of what needed to be done and occupy my hurting mind. Nevertheless, Dad was still miles down the road and there I was in my car with no check boxes to take care of and a battle brewing in my brain about whether all this were really true.

It did not matter. I would be there in just a while and I would put this all to rest when I saw for myself. But, let me just ask God to make her be there. If only He would let her be there, I would see her more often, I swear. I would be better a better son and always, always make those birthday calls and Mother's Day visits. I would never complain again when I actually did show up to spend time with her and Dad, only to hear her tell me she was going out with the girls to play bingo for just a "little" while. Man, that woman loved her some bingo. Did not God know that is Mom were gone, she would be leaving that gaggle of women she runs around with to find the bingo halls on their own? God, let her be there when I pull up and I will be a better son. I promise. Sadly, God does not do that sort of thing. He does not work that way. She must be gone. I know Fernando has a great sense of humor but there is no way he could be that warped as to call me with a sick joke like that. It was just not him. Moreover, he told me she died late last night. This was the next day, so surely there is no mistake that she was gone. I guessed she did not miraculously awaken in the wee hours of the morning.

Anger started to boil in my mind. Dammit, Mom! Why didn't you take better care of yourself? Why didn't you quit smoking when the doctors told you to? Why did you and Dad have to live in that podunk little town with what must have been a backwoods hospital? I am sure those hack doctors were so frickin' inept she had no chance when they brought her in the door. And, how did Dad not know this was coming on? I mean, what the heck? They were together almost every day, all day, side by side in their beloved country store. Was he not paying attention and just let my mother get sick and die? Enough! I had to stop that. Not only was I blaming a man who had spent half a century with my mother, I was starting to speak aloud, and I was pissed. Being angry was not going to bring her back and I had to get a hold of myself somehow. I needed something to do.

Aha! Somehow I remembered I had a job and realized it would be wise if I called my boss to let him know I would be out for awhile. There was a duty I needed to perform and a check box I could cross out. Good. I dialed his telephone number and after he said hello, I was able to get out the words that I was on my way to Luray and did not know how many days I would need to be out because my mother died last night. I typed all the words out here but you must understand my boss' level of interpretation ended right at the beginning of the words "...my mother died last night." There was just far too much of a quiver in my voice and out of nowhere, the overwhelming instinct to cry was welling up inside of me. I fought it hard, though. I was not going to cry on the phone with this man. Number one; he was my boss. Number two; he was another man. I was rather stuck at that point, like a child that had just fallen off the swing, landed on his head really, really, hard and was at that silent point right before the wailing. The result of me trying to hold back my tears must have come across to my boss as if someone had just put a gag in my mouth and nothing came out that did not sound like "mah, mah moh, moh die, die, die...sniffle". As soon as those words came out, I pulled the phone from my ear and immediately tried to push the End Call button straight through the phone as fast as my water-filled eyes could find it. I did not care. It just did not seem to matter. My mom was gone and I was not going to break down on the phone to another man. Let him fire me if he wants. I felt myself sink into the car seat as if someone had just slowly laid a bag of concrete mix in my lap and quite simply realized I no longer cared. It did not matter. My mom was gone. So what if I had been an almost absentee son throughout my adult life? She was my mother. She was always supposed to be there and nothing seemed to matter anymore. I just let go for the rest of the ride and resigned myself to the misery of a child who had lost his mother. I just consciously decided to accept how sorry I felt about myself at that moment because life would never be the same without Mom.

My mother's passing was the first time I had ever actually experienced grief in my life. I was forty years old at the time and had gone through a life devoid of deaths and funerals for anyone relatively close. While it was certainly not something that helped me go through the agony of losing my own son, Jonathan, I can absolutely look back now and realize in a microcosmic sense I went through the textbook five stages of grief just between the time I received the dreaded news and when I arrived at her side. I experienced denial, or disbelief, anger, depression and even tried to bargain with God to have my mother back. Acceptance is the last of the five stages, which I initially thought I had gone through as I was enwrapped within the loving arms of my father, brother and sisters for the two weeks or so leading up to my mother's service. Yet, as honest and somewhat painful it is to write, she was not part of my day-to-day life. I realize many men have their mothers routinely in their lives and I admit now I can only wish I had done the same. Because she was not, however, I returned to my home after the funeral and essentially went about my own life as it was before she passed. Now, I had lost my son. I love my mother, certainly, but the death of my child was life and spirit altering. I had negative emotions about my mother's death that I never let out, but they certainly paled in comparison to those with Jonathan.

On the upper end of the scale, I had deep but unfounded anger for the doctors and hospital staff that had him under their care. I had put my trust and my child's very life in their hands and they betrayed me. I had gut searing guilt knowing my blessed child had looked to me, his father, to be his protector, which was a job I had done valiantly for so many years. I had failed us both. I had promised to keep the monsters and bad guys away, and make sure no one would do him harm. I did not do as promised and surely, I was unfit to have been even called a father to that boy. On the lower yet still sensitive side of the scale, I had lost control of my life as it was supposed to be, as from that point forward nothing, absolutely nothing was ever going to be the same as it was the very day before. Unlike my mother's passing, there would be no return to routine, daily life. Every moment of every day from that point forward was going to be in a direction I did not want as my future. I had played a large, loving role in raising my child through some very tough times for him and watched as he grew into a loving and friendly sixteen-year-old with a slew of loyal friends, some girls on his mind, and a golf game that put mine to shame. Now, there would be no first job after high school he could be proud of, or no wedding to a beautiful young woman who would fall in love with him for his handsome looks and pure innocence. There would be no grandchildren in my future. As selfish as it sounds, it must be said that my very identity had just been stripped away. Being a proud father to that child was everything I was.

All of those incredibly powerful feelings were going through me and set themselves deep down in the very core of my soul. Yet, I felt strongly, instinctively, and without conscious control that those emotions had to be suppressed in order to function in my day-to-day life. Yes, I still had a life to live. If I were to list some of the most important lessons my beautiful Jonathan taught me as we shared this world together, one of the top three would be the importance of living life. In the one book on grieving fathers given to me by my schoolmarm friend, several men who had lost children were interviewed. Although I would like to say it was understandable, I also found it odd and a tad disconcerting that a majority of those men reported an urge or desire to take their own lives in order to be immediately be with their child again. None of them went through with it, of course, and I would rather mark it off to the confusion and loss of control brought on by such powerful and churning emotions inside of each. That is the understandable part I referred to a moment ago. Emotions wrapped up in grief can be that destructive and take us away from the basic strengths we have.

Unfortunately, for me, as well as most men, I had every intention of stuffing those grieving emotions deep inside where no one could see them. Fortunately, and for us all, human emotions cannot be suppressed. Emotions flow through us continually, much like a stream in the forest, maintaining balance and giving life to the natural flora and fauna of our little personal ecosystem. Think of a beaver in nature who decided to come along and build a dam across a stream. Once the normal flow of water is stopped, it builds up behind the dam, floods the surrounding land, and drowns out the living, breathing, and beautiful vegetation. It is not hard to visualize that this destroys and permanently changes a once exquisite, productive, and thriving landscape. That scenario deals with throttling the normal flow of water, but it works incredibly similar to our own human emotions. If you are at all like me, keeping emotions in check because I am a guy, you have a bit of a dam built across your stream already, do you not? Some might say we have placed it at the heart, which is the most vulnerable spot where our emotions might slip out and reveal themselves to others.

One day, however, both unannounced and unexpected, comes the heavy flow of grief brought on by the loss of a child. It pours down inside like Noah's forty days and forty nights. You can bet that when it comes those emotional waters will surge downstream towards that dam like a rampant flash flood, roiling, frothing, and following its natural outward path. It will meet the blockage, and for a time flood backwards to drown out and destroy the environment even more. What is being submerged is self-esteem, confidence, a desire to live, relationships with friends, family, and more, all part of a once thriving and beautiful persona. The pressure will continue to build and emotional waters rise until the dam is eventually overrun and blown apart, exploding as if made of twigs and leafs. The result will be an escaping cascade of raging, raw emotions rushing frenzied downstream and outwards towards others, destroying everything it comes in contact with, including any remaining friendships, passions and the potential for an amazing life. It is obvious to recognize the destruction.

My dam was strong, too. My little grief beaver committed an incredible feat of emotional engineering and built a structure that held back the floodwaters for quite some time. Make no mistake, as the powerful emotions continued to build and the larger the dammed up flooding became, the more the impact affected my life inside and out. If any good can be found from this, at least for myself, mine burst and there was much destroyed, but my emotional stream now runs more freely. I am certainly not completely clear of the blockage, but I am working on that. My little eco-persona, once flooded and dying behind the dam has somewhat come back to life, and I am slowly repairing what the flood destroyed when it raged outwards in my life with the burst. My barrier came down without warning, albeit in my shower where I could constantly return to and have some level of control of the flow as it exposes itself to others. And, what of my industrious little beaver? Well, I have a pelt on my wall and I am keeping an eye out for any of his little family and friends.

Large toothed, furry mammals aside, part of my personal goals along the path to healing was to study and understand emotions as they relate to humans in general. I wondered why they were such a driving part of our life and why it was so very difficult to control them. After all, holding them in was my natural urge, as my initial studies in male emotions told me, and it was just another acceptable part of my anatomy, right? In reality, what I came to realize is the entire mess is actually a double-edged sword. Weak or strong, emotions are a basic requirement for humans, and are pure primal instinct in nature, actually just as essential to life as our heart beating and lungs pumping. We do not have to tell our heart to beat, nor lungs to breathe air, as this all takes place on a subconscious level. We literally need not think to make those things happen. In large part, we do not consciously have to tell our emotions to work for us either. I was surprised to find our emotions are a leading factor in every decision-making process in our daily lives, regardless of personal, professional or pleasure. For years, I was taught never to make business decisions based off my emotions, as the industry leaders preached logic and reason as the only acceptable driving factor for success. What my finding uncovered, however, was emotions are actually the rudimentary, base element in every choice, whether Carnegie, Ford, or Getty ever wanted to admit it.

To illustrate while trying to maintain my vow to avoid citing dry, mundane research, I will simply tell you about a modern day neuroscientist named Antonio Damasio. He recently conducted extensive studies of a large group of patients who had suffered an injury or other impairment to the brain that eliminated their ability to feel emotions. Much like Mr. Spock of the Star Ship Enterprise, while they were bereft of emotions, all other manners of their mind functioned properly, including reason and logic. Unlike science fiction characters from the planet Vulcan, however, the research patient's lack of emotions kept them from making even the simplest of decisions. During failed attempts, the patients could use and tell of their logic and reasoning processes, but were unable to come to a concluding selection in every single effort. As a quick example, when offered a choice of fish or chicken for a meal, the patient could not pick between the two. Why? There was no ability to determine the "reward/punishment" outcome, a term used by the good neurologist. Fish or chicken, of course, was a very simple example, just the same as defining reward/punishment as the result of either being happy or sad with a final choice. Yet, that is what it comes down to instinctively. Will a decision bring happiness in some way? You can define happiness in many terms, as well. After all, we may never have developed into a species if early Homo sapiens allowed the reward for food, which made them happy, to override the unhappy punishment of death if they just walked up to their intended prey bare handed. If that were the case, early man would have ended as greasy blots on the hooves of Mastodons and tasty treats for the Sabretooth. In the same manner, contemplate reward and punishment in the very odd man who somewhere, sometime in our past plucked an oyster from the shore and for the first time decided, "I'm going to eat this just the way it is." What was he thinking?

While I felt a strong need to dive in deeply to the study of general emotions and then the specific emotional response of men, there seemed to be less real life studies of "grief" related emotions than I would have supposed. Many of the formal definitions of grief are similar to the following: "Grief is the normal and natural emotional reaction to loss or change of any kind." Okay, so grief is an emotional reaction only, right? Well, the overreaching common definition of emotion is the following: "Emotions are the temporary feelings subject to change with surrounding circumstances." Well, I can tell you from experience that some of my feelings are not so temporary. We are not referring to normal life where little Cindy becomes sad because it began to rain and she had to come inside. She will remain sad until something else catches her attention or the rain ceases, at which time her emotion of sadness will end because something else took her attention or she returned outdoors. Her emotion was temporary and was affected by changing surroundings. Yet, ask any father who lost a child, regardless of how many years or decades ago it was and you will find that some of the "emotional" elements or feelings of grief continue. Further, there are no activities or changing circumstances that will remove the sadness or replace the loss. More importantly, grief from child loss is actually made up of many very powerful emotions. Yet in my opinion, not all of them are bad. Absolutely some are destructive and must be dealt with before they have incredibly negative impacts on us. Guilt, as I spoke of in another chapter, is usually unfounded and a very common emotion in our loss, but can have no positive effect on our lives.

Although I had no reason whatsoever to know the following days would result in the loss of my child, I felt so much grief in some of the words and actions I referred to earlier. I know now I was feeling false guilt as well as the baseless anger I initially felt for the hospital staff, and allowed that and so much more to flood behind my dam. Sorrow, on the other hand, will never leave me. The day I no longer feel a level of sadness, longing and ache for the loss of my wonderful son is the day my heart has turned to stone. I will always feel sadness because he is no longer with me, and to those who tell me he is in a better place, I respectfully say they are wrong. Yes, I am convinced he is surrounded by unconditional love and either fishing with my father or teaching him how to play video games. Yes, I know that there could be no truer "better" place than being in Heaven beside the Lord, but in a better place for me? No. Believe me, I take a lot of solace in knowing his spirit lives, yet the better place for me would be right here by my side, tossing the football and avoiding discussions of his poor math grades. Regardless, grief, wrapped in those evil, destructive emotions that must not in any way become permanent in your soul, have to be addressed. They are a powerful human instinct and flow through you like a river looking to return to the sea. As men, we have dammed up that river long before the real "storm" came upon us and if, like me, you cannot take the advice to seek professional help, find your "shower" and break down your dam before it destroys you. It will change the rest of your life.

The Humility of Why

"If pain doesn't lead to humility, you have wasted your suffering."
~ Katerina Stoykova Klemer

Jonathan entered my world and humbled me. That newborn child reintroduced humility to my life just as gently as an avalanche introduces itself to a snow skier. Only a day after he was born his mother and I found ourselves trying to follow a speeding ambulance from the suburbs of Northern Virginia into the urban craziness of Washington, DC, as I blew through red traffic lights and avoided at least a half dozen narrow escapes with other cars. Not much earlier that same day, we had been advised by the doctors at Alexandria Hospital that our beautiful, seemingly healthy baby boy had entered the world without a fully functioning heart. The left side, we were told, did not develop in the womb and because of that, he might not survive through even that night. While that would bring anyone to their knees, it was actually not the humbling part. I was far too much in shock at that point to be humbled in any way. Jonathan had been born just the day before, and we hugged and held that little bundle of joy until he was unexpectedly whisked away once the physical symptoms of his fragile condition became obvious to an alert nurse.

After a team of on-staff pediatric doctors fully evaluated my child, I was told of the option to have Jonathan transferred immediately to Children's Hospital. I voiced my immediate say-so almost before the doctor even finished getting the words out of his mouth. He went on, however, to explain that while they could keep him there at the local hospital, Children's was far better suited to deal with his severe cardiac condition. His poor mother, however, had her own post-delivery condition. She had just delivered Jonathan the day before by Cesarean Section, and was originally slated to remain in recovery for a few days before we would go home with my new little buddy. I certainly understood that, as I was there and saw that little jaw dropping procedure go down. She felt not an ounce of pain while laid back on the operating table and calmly spoke of wall colors for the baby's room, bills due, or whatever came to mind. We could have been at the kitchen table and talked over coffee from the way she casually acted. Curiosity got the better of me for a moment, though, and I decided to a little look-see at what was going on. Her hospital gown had been lifted at the bottom and attached to a wire above the table in order to block her own view of the procedure, but I bravely peeked around it, yet absolutely not for very long. I had no idea what to expect but what I witnessed appeared as if the doctors had raised the hood on a 71' Chevy Chevelle and were elbow deep in pulling out an engine. That day I saw parts of my wife I do not think any husband is supposed to see, or wants to see, so I snapped my head back to her side of the gown and uttered a naive, "oops."

I made the immediate decision to transfer Jonathan to Children's Hospital just the day after that massive invasion of my wife's innards had taken place. Because of that, I fully expected the medical staff on hand to tell my wife she would have to stay and continue her own recovery before she could be discharged to join me. Bless their hearts, though, as that was not even considered an option. Instead, they quickly bundled, bandaged, and medicated Jonathan's mother to the moon and out the door we went. We fortunately had just enough time to get to our car and pulled up behind the ambulance as newborn Jonathan was brought out in a clear, glass like box on wheels. Through the box, I could see he was already burdened with intravenous lines, as well as vital stat leads that ran to monitors hung on portable, wheeled poles. At that point, it had been hours since he was taken from my arms and I wanted nothing more than to climb inside of that ambulance to ride at his side so it was no wonder time seemed to come to a standstill as we sat in our car and waited to get underway. Yet, I knew from my own background as a cop that it takes a few minutes to stabilize a patient for the ride, and with my delicate newborn baby, that was just fine with me. I had actually anticipated a long, slow ride into DC, which I would be grateful for, not only for little Jonathan but because I had no idea where we were going. The hospital staff had certainly given me the address to Children's Hospital but in my state of mind, it meant nothing in those days before car equipped GPS navigation. I would need to be led.

Soon, it would become obvious I was way off base when I predicted a long, slow run into Washington, DC when the ambulance driver decided it was time to go. Apparently, he had not been told, nor cared, that we were following, and obviously intended to take full advantage of his emergency lights and siren. Regardless, there was no way he would lose me. I had been on my share of high speed pursuits in my day and had never been left behind. There was no way a paramedic was going to be my first, whether I was chasing in a police cruiser or not. I will not detail all the traffic violations I committed as I remained on his tail, but other than being my guide along the way, it would all be for not. When we pulled into the emergency entrance right behind the ambulance, I was immediately told to park in the regular parking lot and come in through the main entry. That was not what I wanted to hear. I wanted to follow Jonathan directly in to wherever they were taking him, but at this point, I was too numb to do anything but follow orders. I was in a different world and almost too scared to be aggressive or assertive, so off to the parking lot I went.

Once Jonathan's mother and I were inside, a nurse met us at the information desk and escorted us through numerous hallways and down at least two different elevators before we came to a door with a narrow window. The nurse informed us that Jonathan was inside with the doctors and we could take a seat in some nearby chairs and wait for the doctors to come out and speak. I was not going to sit, of course, and was taken slightly aback as I peered through the window into the well-lit room. It seemed like only seconds since I had parked the car, although time was really not measurable to me at that point, and already there were at least nine masked and gowned individuals that surrounded the blanketed table where I assumed my son laid. While I could not see him for the crowd, I felt slightly better that there was so much instant attention being paid to my son. Only a few moments later I noticed one of the doctors across the table had looked up and noticed me, at which point he turned his head to one side, and then the other and I could see his mask move as he spoke to the others in the huddle. After just a moment or so, the entire group began to move from around the table and towards the door.

It is odd what you remember during times of high emotions but to me they appeared to all move as one single unit, almost as if they were several parts of the same form. To this day, I am not even sure if their feet shuffled or they just collectively glided to and through the door, where they met me in the hallway. Surgical masks were lowered then, and I witnessed a combination of old white men, not so old Middle Eastern men, one or two women and one kid who I could not believe was even out of high school, much less medical school. Someone spoke and thank goodness I only saw one mouth move, as everything seemed overly nightmarish and surreal enough already. I thought then the speaker must be the doctor in charge. However, I would later learn that the brains of these mobile, symbiotic-like medical consortiums that roamed from room to room seldom have the senior member act as the spokesman of the group. Instead, someone junior generally "presents" so that the senior can judge performance. Over sixteen years I would learn much about how hospitals operated, no pun intended. Regardless, I was told very compassionately of Jonathan's life threatening heart condition and that although he was not out of the immediate woods, they felt he could be stabilized for the time being and then evaluated for consideration for a fairly new cardiac procedure that would help his little, deformed heart. We would just have to wait while they tested and observed over the next several days.

Over the upcoming days, I likened myself to Viktor Navorski, the Tom Hanks character from the movie Terminal. Oh, I could have left the building if I wanted to, but there was no way I would allow myself. If I could not be beside Jonathan while he was being tended to, I would wait where I could run back to him every time it was okay to do so. During those anxious times, though, I wandered any and every hallway, alleyway, passageway, outhouse, henhouse, and well, never mind, in Children's Hospital. I could do no more than wait for people I did not even know a few hours before to tell me if I would have the future I thought I had just the day before. Was I despondent? You bet! I just remember so many thoughts about poor, poor me. Woe is me. How could I have a child with a heart defect?" I was a Kelly and dammit, Kellys were healthy and strong. This could not be right, could it? Moreover, this poor child, my baby, what kind of life will he have? I was told they might be able to give him a two-chamber heart that would work well enough and keep him alive, but why, oh why does he have to come in to this world with such a burden? It just was not fair to him. With all those thoughts swirling through my mind, I despaired, face down in my anguish and shuffled my feet through miles and miles of hospital hallways feeling like life was just totally unfair to me and to my child.

In my wanderings, I happened to look around for no other reason than to abandon zombie mode long enough to take in my surroundings. The first thing I noticed was that I was outside of a common area playroom with floor to ceiling windows that fully allowed anyone to see the activities. My ears brought my focus to a particular child having fun and laughing loudly in that contagious kind of way that makes you instinctively want to join in. He was on the lap of whom I assumed was his mother who pulled at a drawstring attached to a big, chunky toy helicopter. Each time she pulled the string, the two wooden propellers on top spun while the highly amused child threw his head back and broke out in pure, gleeful pleasure. I could not help but smile my own infectious smile. After a few moments, I also could not help but be jealous, too. There before my eyes was a happy mother and her baby who enjoyed the joyous time together that only a parent and child could have. I only prayed to have those experiences someday with my son, who at that moment was not completely assured of even hearing his own laughter. That terrible notion caused me to drop my head and stare at the carpet in despair when that cheerful and precious child broke out in another fit of laughter. I once again uncontrollably smiled and looked back at the boy, but this time caught a view I had not noticed before. The toddler was on his mother's lap all right, but he was not sitting at all. That gleeful, blissful baby was actually missing both legs and instead of sitting, was instead just placed carefully in his mommy's lap and tilted back against her body. In fact, it appeared to me that he was missing more than just his legs. Even though he was dressed in toddler clothes, the aspect I was able to view made it seem like his upper torso ended somewhere just below his belly button. Lord, he looked so happy, though. Yet, how could he be? How could his mother be so happy? That child was missing both of his legs, at least and I felt so very, very sad for them.

As I scanned the well-lit and brightly colored playroom, I noticed other groups of parents and children, as well. Some had obvious maladies, while you could not tell what circumstance or condition brought the others. Regardless, everyone in the room seemed to teem with one common characteristic; the children happily went about playtime as if all was normal in their world. I also recognized that although they appeared strong in front of their kids, life for those loving parents was not going to be what they had obviously envisioned before. For the children, however, at this point in their lives they absolutely seemed to know life was not meant to be any different from what it was. I would see this repeated throughout each hallway, it seemed, and for the first time started taking quick glances into open patient rooms of other children in the hospital. Sometimes the rooms were bright and cheery, with groups of people inside, and my quick glances were oblivious to them. Other rooms were dark and quiet, usually with mom and dad types sitting quietly beside a hospital bed or crib. As I walked by, often the parents looked out towards me and smile weakly and I would look back and return the unspoken greeting. I began to understand that I was not alone in my pain of being the parent to a special child and the thought brought back something my mother had said many times in her years; No matter how bad you think you have it, someone else always has it worse. I realized I was incredibly selfish, as well. How much of this time had I concentrated on how bad I had it? Of course, I was frightened that my little child would not make it but how much thought had I really given to him? Of course, I wanted him to have a healthy heart with no limitations through his life. If he could not have one, though, would a two-chamber heart be just as normal to him as four? I understood then how blessed I would be if he survived, as I would have a child with two arms and two legs and who would walk, talk, and play. There I was in a hospital where it was obvious that these children with heartbreaking medical conditions seemed to be just as happy as any child, and I was humbled by the lesson each had given me.

Jonathan himself also had so much more to teach me about being humble. To my amazing joy, he did survive his second night in this world and went on to undergo three open-heart surgeries before the age of two and a half to reconstruct his underdeveloped heart. The entire procedure had to be broken up into separate surgeries since each would be extensively difficult and put a great amount of strain on his delicate system. It was after his first open-heart I would realize his awesome instinctual will to live. He knew no different. In his post-surgery recovery crib, I saw Jonathan quietly lying in a medical coma, the pain too excruciating for him to be allowed to waken. He had a breathing tube down his throat, IV lines pushing and pulling fluids almost everywhere you could imagine, bandages covering him like pajamas, as well as miles of tape and monitoring lines. My child was such a tiny and helpless little thing to have to go through so much. The surgeon's Physician's Assistant joined me at bedside and compassionately explained the surgery and the risks, and as gently as she could, warned me that Jonathan was in very real danger, especially during that recovery period. If we would lose him, it would be during that time when his body was reacting to all the trauma needed just to get inside to hopefully save his life. If all went well, however, he would be in the Pediatric Intensive Care Unit, or the PICU, for at least four to six weeks where he would be monitored and observed at all times. I know it was only a few short days before I looked down into the crib at a cooing, seemingly happy infant, obviously unaware of his peril. Almost miraculously, Jonathan recovered well ahead of schedule and after the third week, the doctors proclaimed he was doing great and we were blissfully sent packing for home.

Each of Jonathan's next two open-heart surgeries went fantastic, as well, and he recovered much quicker and healthier than expected. After both successive procedures, his precious heart exceeded the expectations of his doctors and functioned completely in line with what everyone involved wanted to see medically. After the third and final open-heart procedure, Jonathan's surgeon, the amazing man who saved his life, would come out of the operating room with a moment of time to speak. When I asked him what was next for my son, his response took the weight of the world off my shoulders. The doctor answered that he would look at Jonathan later in life and if he needed any additional work, it would be easy to take care of. I could not have heard sweeter words. I had a son who was going to live, and I was overjoyed to say the least. I was also not lost on the fact that over the past two and a half years our lives had been enveloped in either life threatening surgeries with extensive and nerve wracking recovery, or the anxiety and worry of scheduled surgeries to come. There is little to compare with the heartbreak over the past few years when I brought that infant child to the hospital. There he would be in my arms, beautiful and bundled, while he smiled and laughed with his goofy father. Each time he was completely unaware of the train wreck I was about to submit him to. After that third and final reconstruction, blessedly we had no surgeries scheduled for the foreseeable future and could take a breath.

I wrote the words we had no surgeries scheduled, and you might think to chastise me because it was not I who experienced those incredibly tough open-heart surgeries, was it? In fact, my precious little child was the one who unwillingly submitted to the danger and pains of having his chest and heart remodeled, not me. Yet, it was so very tough on me as well, as it would have been on any loving parent. That was my child, my responsibility, and for whom I felt unconditional love. I would have traded myself on those operating tables and in those recovery beds in the blink of an eye. Through every medical procedure that child went through, I suffered immensely in anxiety, fear, and feelings of helplessness. Just like Jonathan, though, I would recover each time, with full credit to being humbled by that child's amazing will to survive. To witness what he went through as an infant child completely changed my whole aspect on the instinct to live. I wondered often, since I had so much time to think while I sat beside his crib during recoveries, what I would have been like as an adult who experienced the same thing. Would I have handled it as well? Would the day-to-day troubles of life, bringing with it concerns about bills, the job, and just whatever, sap my constitution and strength to make it through recovery? For Heaven's sake, I cannot even imagine submitting myself to an open-heart surgery without at least milking it for several months of sympathy from those around me. Yet, not that kid. Every time I looked at him, I saw an innocent child, too young to form even logical thought, who instinctively knew only one thing: I am supposed to live. I am supposed to be alive! He had absolutely no knowledge of the danger he was in, and his mind was unencumbered with the fret and worry we cart around with us every day as adults. His body knew nothing else at that time but to heal and to survive, and when it instinctively told him it was time to get up, he simply did and moved on with his life.

Jonathan's quick and miraculous recovery was, of course, to the detriment of the PICU nurses on duty during his frequent stays. They often reverted to threats of being tied to his crib if he continued to bounce up and down for hours on end. At just the age of two and a half this little man would often pick up one of the miniature footballs I always brought for him, and used absolute perfect timing as he nailed any poor, unsuspecting nurse who happened to be walking by his door. During the end of that third recovery, just as I was beginning to think in the back of my mind that Jonathan could be "sprung" soon, his attending physician decided to give my little man a look over to see how he was doing. He first scanned through the recent entries into Jonathan's records, which were stacked on the small table beside his crib. Jonathan did not have medical charts. He had binders, and several of them, each at least three inches thick. Regardless, as the doctor laid down the binder in his hands, he leaned into the crib to playfully put his face against Jonathan's when my little stinker grabbed the doctor by his tie and threw himself backwards onto the mattress, effectively pulling the doctor's head down inside the crib with him. Without missing a beat, the good doctor turned his head up to me, smiled, and said, "Yeah. We had better get him out of here before the nurses kill him."

The years went by and Jonathan grew in leaps and bounds, yet with some other medical events here and there. Because there was so much scar tissue on the surface of his heart, the pathway that controlled the correct impulses to beat had been slightly retarded. To help, an internal pacemaker was put in immediately following the third and final rebuild procedure. Therefore, as he grew there would be frequent pacemaker changes when the battery would run low and another major open-heart surgery to replace the wires where they were connected to the heart. He also had his tonsils and adenoids removed to combat sleep apnea and the three heart caths in his teen years. Yet, through each, except for the final heart cath that would take him away from me, Jonathan continued to show the same humbling instinct to recover, live, and be happy. While he was skipping through life, having a ball, I accepted a business development position with a security firm headquartered in Germany and worked from a home office, which afforded me the ability to spend more time with Jonathan and some incredibly fond years of driving my child back and forth to school each day. As you can probably imagine, he and I had some remarkable father-son times during those daily shuttles and I will cherish them forever. The job also afforded me the ability to work from anywhere I wanted, as well. Therefore, in 2007, we escaped the madness of the DC Metro area, with all its traffic, crime, and problems, and relocated to

Northern Mississippi near the Le Bonheur Children's Hospital in Memphis, Tennessee. The hospital is internationally renowned for their leading edge pediatric cardiology programs and a neighbor of Saint Jude's Children's Research Hospital, founded by Danny Thomas, and focusing exclusively on children with cancer.

Saint Jude's is a rather vast facility, or campus really, with an exceptionally large security program outsourced to a private security company. Sometime after I moved to the area, Saint Jude's had decided to solicit bids for that service, as they looked to see if they could get either better service or a better cost, or both, and I decided to submit a bid. As part of the whole process, the administration would conduct a tour of the facility so bidders would be able to see the program in action and have a better idea of the needs. I really looked forward to a walk-through of that magic place, so well known for curing children of such a nasty, horrible thing as cancer. I had seen my share of cancer in adults, but most were older, including my father who was taken with a form of that horrible disease. Cancer that dared to attack children, however, seemed so much more treacherous in my heart. Although I had never visited the hospital before, I had seen so many advertisements and attended frequent Saint Jude funded events. The often-touted success stories made me think of just how encouraging it must be if, sadly, you had a child with cancer but got to Saint Jude's. If so, your child would live and all would be right in the world again.

When the time came to tour the facilities of St. Jude's, I had fully anticipated and mentally prepared my heart to seeing the children who were undergoing treatment at the time. I had become very accustomed to hospital environments and not being a rookie at the whole thing, never expected being humbled again. I had warned myself in advance that depending on where the tour took us, I might see heart tugging young cancer patients without hair, as this was a pretty common image displayed in telethons and charity events. Yet, I was absolutely sure I would be walking into a laboratory type facility, almost like a Sci-Fi movie setting. After all, the battle with cancer required serious men and women in lab coats and children carefully isolated in germ free glass rooms, right? Keep in mind, I had been in Children's Hospital in DC, as well as Le Bonheur Children's Hospital there in Memphis. I knew that both went well out of the way to create a wonderful and happy environment for the kids. However, fighting cancer in children was a serious battle, and in my mind, Saint Jude's was the champion. Surely, there would be no fluff there. It would be sterile, somber and down to business, surely.

Regardless, the tour started out in their vast, open, and welcoming lobby. Right away, I noticed children of all ages, with the telltale shaved heads, as they roamed freely in and out of the connecting hallways and cafeteria. It was obvious these were young patients. The hospital's internal head of security began his brief and soon we were walking down hallways as brightly lit and as colorful as you could imagine with artwork and wonderful drawings everywhere. There were visibly happy children everywhere, as well. Some were walking with medical staff, some with probable parents, siblings, or friends, and everyone seemed so merry. Even as the tour continued by patient rooms, to look inside any of them, you would have thought there had been a fire alarm. There were no kids in bed. Apparently, they were all in the hallways, smiling as they walked to or from somewhere, or in one of the many media centers, activity or playrooms we passed in our tour. I was used to kids in hospitals, though, and in the back of my mind just knew there were areas where kids were going through, or had just gone through some dangerous procedure. Yet, for the moment, all I witnessed was an atmosphere so far and away from what I had pictured before I arrived.

While the sight of these ill but outwardly cheerful kids was incredibly humbling in itself, the tour soon brought us to an area I had never actually seen in my days, or frankly, actually never thought of. We would not have been taken there as part of the tour had it not been for the need to see the security guard station that controlled access to and from the area behind the slightly tinted glass doors. We were at the entrance to the "Palliative Care" area of the hospital, which was both an unfamiliar word and concept in my life. Thank goodness, someone else in the tour spoke up and asked what those words meant. It was explained to all of us in a fittingly solemn manner that not all cancer could be cured, and the palliative care section of the hospital was where those children with incurable cancer were comforted until they succumbed to their horrible conditions. I was simply, humbly floored by those words. Many times I had casually considered the mortality of my own son, but had effectively dealt with that by knowing he had gone through so much and always came out stronger. That day at Saint Jude's, however, I stood at those glass doors and began to realize just how very blessed I actually was. I had my child, no matter what he had been through to live. Yet, not every child survives, and that thought began to swirl around my mind.

The tour was certainly not going to take us inside the sensitive and private area, but while the head of security advised the tour group of the guard's duty, I just could not stop looking through the glass. As I did, a door just beyond the darkened glass opened and a young man walked out and came in our direction. The door he departed, obviously controlled by a self-closing mechanism, started its long, slow return, but it was not fast enough to stop the image of a very young girl, maybe five or six, and what must have been her mother sitting together on a bed inside. They both talked and smiled the light through their room window allowed me to witness the mother tying a beautiful pink bandana around this sweet child's head. I could not take my eyes away until the door closed completely, but just as it did, the young man walked by and continued past the glass through which I openly gawked. He caught my eye and he actually gave a brief smile as he walked on to wherever his destination was, while a second and much more powerful surge of humility almost knocked me to my knees. I thought I had gone to the brink and back with my child, having lived through the gut wrenching anxiety of so many surgeries. I had heard too often that Jonathan might not make it through the night. No parent could have gone through the level of multiple nightmares I had and I certainly had earned the right to say I knew humility. Yet, I had my son, did I not? No matter what I had gone through to that point, I had always taken my son home. Yet, right there on the other side of that glass door were parents who knew that one day, and possibly soon, they would not be taking their child home. I had no idea how many more rooms there were or how many other parents who would spend the final days, or maybe even hours with the greatest gift in their lives. Only one room, however, and only one child I knew then to be terminal was enough to put an instant, life changing reemphasize on the concept that no matter how bad I thought I had it, truly, someone else had it worse. God bless though parents and children.

Why me? Why my child? Those are very, very powerful questions, and ones with no real answer. They are questions we will never allow another to answer for us, either. No comment of, "It was God's will," or "It was his time," is ever going to help solve the mystery for me, no matter how well intended. Even though I am a devout believer in God and His words within the Bible, I personally do not believe it is against His will to ask. Yet, I am also aware that I may not be enlightened to his answer until I am indeed by his side. For the time being, I will have to live with the humilities of life and realize I am not alone in my loss. I am not the only parent to lose a child. As hard as it sounds, I have to tell myself "why not my child?" I think of the many, many children who are taken from us every day by illness, disease or some senseless accident or event. I also think of the many young men and woman who have lost their lives in defense of our country. Far too many of those brave service members were just kids as well, and barely over the age of eighteen. My own son was just a couple years younger than those heroes who gave all, and you can bet their parents are still asking the anguishing question of why as well. While there may be no real answer on this earth for the loss of a child, I have been greatly aided by remembering the humilities of Jonathan's sheer will to survive, as well as other events that I was exposed to along the way. I am not the only father who sadly lost a loving child. Nor, am I the only father who will be joyously humbled when someday I hold my beautiful baby boy so very tightly in my arms again.

Tbe Normalcy Bias

"Landing on the shores of normalcy is wonderful, especially after being tossed around in the sea of sickness."

~ *Khang Kijarro Nguyen*

It was nippy that morning in the lobby of Le Bonheur Children's Hospital. Jonathan and I sat at one of the small, round kid's tables, each of us face down in our smartphones as we silently tried to keep our minds off what was coming. I read work emails, and Jonathan watched videos or scanned social media or something, as he tried all the while to not reveal how nervous and scared he was. I knew he was, of course, but I also knew that bringing it up again, as I had already reassured him several times that morning, would just elicit another retort that he was okay. Besides, I might take away the concentration needed to keep up his facade of braveness. Instead, when we occasionally took our faces away from the phones, we talked of things that would go on for the next few weeks, since summer time was upon us. The swimming pool was cleaned, filled, and ready for backyard fun. Jonathan's golf game was going wonderfully, fueled by the generosity of a client of mine. The client had just given Jonathan a full set of the same golf clubs used by one of the most popular golf pros on tour and my son was the talk of our golf course neighborhood. There was much to look forward to after his latest heart catheterization was behind him.

It was very, very early on June 12, 2013, and we had already checked in with the receptionist at the desk. Jonathan was scheduled to have a relatively simple heart cath where the pediatric surgeon would enter the artery inside his left thigh and travel up to the heart in order to tie off the blood vessels I referred to earlier as collaterals veins, or cheaters in my terms. Whatever they were called, they robbed my son's heart of oxygen rich blood and had to be taken care of. Soon we would be escorted back to pre-op, the cath operation would be performed, and then Jonathan would be taken straight to the Pediatric ICU for recovery. He was already scheduled to stay at least overnight, but if he recovered quickly the next day, which he always did, he would be discharged for home for several days of lazily flopping around the house. At the time, the biggest threat to Jonathan was his start of summer fun. Just as it was with his last cath, afterwards he would not be allowed to submerge his leg in water for several days, nor would he be allowed to swing a golf club for at least two weeks. Instead, he would be tortured with the view of the pool and the golf course beyond as he peered from the couch through the window. The cath incision had to be given time to heal completely and if it were to be reopened, the results would be rather messy and probably not good.

That morning, as we waited for the surgery to get underway, we were both nervous. For me, however, nerves were there, but took a backseat to the fact we had been through the same thing so many times before. I just wanted to get on the other side of the whole day and take my son home the next. For me, I would be put out with a couple days off work and an uncomfortable chair to sleep in throughout the night at Jonathan's bedside. Soon enough, though, Jonathan was called back and after a delay for an unscheduled emergency surgery, was wheeled from the pre-op area back to the cath-lab, as it is called, with a kiss on his forehead and a "see you soon, buddy" from his dad. I watched as the surgical staff pushed his gurney towards the final corner and as he took one more look back my way, I raised my hand and flashed, "I love you" in sign language. That gesture had become our way of communicating love from across a distance over the years, or just whenever saying it aloud was not appropriate. Sometimes we also did it just to do it, regardless when or where. From his gurney, Jonathan flashed I love you back as I noticed the anxiety build in face. Before I could come up with some expression of assurance, he was wheeled around the corner, gone from my sight and I would never see my wonderful baby boy awake again.

Until that dreadful morning in June, I had lived within the realm of what has been termed by psychologists as the Normalcy Bias. One of the most commonly accepted definitions of this is "A mental state entered by persons facing a potential disaster, causing underestimation of both the possibility and its after effects, many times resulting in situations where people fail to adequately prepare." The term has almost been completely hijacked by the government now, as I discovered when I attempted to read multiple research publications on the topic. While it is a human trait, modern study seems to equate it more so towards entire communities of people, including such places as

New Orleans, the State of California or other geographic areas where the potential for natural disaster is high. The government uses the studies to gear the leaders within a populous to be prepared for the potential of disaster at all times, while the inhabitants seem to go about life as if nothing could ever go wrong. Almost understandably, many find it so much easier to just live in a blissful state of denial. As for me, I could relate to it on a personal level, as my normalcy bias focused around my son, Jonathan, and the sincere belief that he would always be there. At the very moment I lost him, I became shocked and traumatized. Although I had always been aware that he had been born with a life threatening heart defect and even the simplest of surgeries carried a degree of risk to his life, I had no real expectation that he could pass away. Some might presume, however, that due to my son's condition I should not claim the same level of "Post Traumatic Stress" as those who lost a child without warning. Yet, absolutely nothing could be farther from the truth. I existed happily within the normalcy bias, content and falsely secure that life would always go on with my son at my side until the fateful day I left this earth first.

Without question, when it comes to the loss of a child, no two experiences will be alike and no one could ever speak to anyone's specific suffering after such a devastating event. When it came to Jonathan, I only expected normal for his life and losing him was honestly never a consideration in my thoughts or in his future. Was being unprepared actually my fault or did I want to believe it so strongly that I allowed it to be planted there by my own tricky mind? I know now it was my mind, as I go back to when, as just a toddler,

Jonathan survived his third and final open-heart procedure. Immediately afterwards his miracle-working surgeon told me Jonathan was out of the woods and without a lot of drama stated that he would look at my son sometime further down the road and tweak anything that needed tweaking. That was all that mattered to me then, and my mind soaked in those words as if they were much wanted and needed food for my soul. No matter what, that man had provided a conviction in my mind that my son was always going to be okay. Jonathan also helped bolster my convictions, as he championed each and every earlier surgery in his life, defying the odds at times, and flourished. That created a basic level of faith within me that he was intended to be here forever, and his death, even though he went through so much, was not a real concern.

The mind can be very powerful and crafty, sometimes tricking us with good results, and sometimes with results not so good. The trickster part generally lives way back in the subconscious mind and often makes itself known without being asked to step forward. During my years as a security director, I became involved in firearms instruction, teaching armed security guards how to properly handle, shoot, and store their service weapons. When it came to discussions of street survival, I would target the effects of television and movies on our subconscious responses to live situations. In these normally graphic and dramatic shoot em' ups, whoever was on the unlucky end of the shot would dramatically fly backwards through the air before saying something profound or profane, and then just simply keel over and die. On the screen, that scenario happens far more times than not and with constant visual repetition, our minds fervently believe that if shot we are supposed to die. It is in the script, right? To counter this, I showed each class a training film that showed actual recorded footage of a heavy shootout. The firefight was between several FBI agents and a bad guy, whom they promptly filled with seventy-seven bullet holes during the melee. The firefight took place over the course of three or four minutes while the bad guy aggressively advanced on their positions while taking round after round to his body. He would have continued too, had his body not actually run completely out of blood, which poured from him like water through a spaghetti strainer and his heart had no option but to stop. Apparently, he never watched television and was therefore blindly ignorant to the fact he was supposed to die after the first shot.

As an additional part of my firearms training and conditioned thoughts, I also highlighted the power of the mind as I provided a personal experience where the subconscious implanting of a thought had been placed in my mind. I was given the thought implant at a time my emotions were high, which I know played a large role in the way my mind was open to it. At the age of three, I was admitted to a hospital to have my tonsils removed after I had experienced back-to-back bouts of strep throat. Understand that back in the sixties, if you came down with tonsillitis, they just ripped those babies out. It was just what they did back then. While it is not normal for a toddler to recall memories so clearly, I can tell you I do remember that hospital stay like it went down last week. I was more concerned about not knowing what was going on than being afraid, as I had been taken from my home, carried into a strange building, and then placed in a bed where people I did not know stood around and talked about me. I also remember that I got myself out of bed, took my clothes from the tall metal locker against the wall, dressed myself, and headed out the room door. Fortunately, given my age, I lacked the stealthy skills needed to make my escape, as I attempted to walk right by the doctor and my parents just outside. I was quickly wrangled, of course, and put back into bed, where for the rest of the evening I was enchanted with stories of the copious amounts of ice cream I would be allowed to eat. The doctors recommended it, I was told, since it was good for the throat after my tonsils were gone. I also recall that I sat up in the hospital bed as my father handed over a small stack of comic books and became sad when I realized I could not read the words. Thankfully, comics were filled with pictures, and as most guys will tell you, pictures are really what we are after in our periodicals.

In those days of yore, young patients such as me who would undergo tonsillectomies were admitted the evening prior and allowed to fall asleep on their own. Then, early in the morning before the child woke naturally, he or she would be put under with anesthesia and the surgery performed. Just as I neared sleep that night, the doctor came into my room and spent a few minutes as he talked to my mom and dad before he came to my bedside. I still recall his face as he leaned close to mine and told me he understood my throat hurt very badly but he was going to take care of that. He went on to say distinctly that in the morning he would remove my tonsils and make it so "…you will never have another sore throat." That was it. He told me that I would never have another sore throat. I awoke the next day after the tonsils were removed and was not sure anything had happened at all. My mother and father were there, of course, and a nurse who told me she knew I just had to be in terrible pain but I could have some ice cream soon to help. I was not in pain, however, and actually no longer felt the pain I had when I got there. I was a little confused and if not for the adult to baby pep talk about being such a brave boy, I would have been nervous that the whole thing was still to come. It was over, however, and I accepted the ice cream when the time came, not to ease the pain, but more so because I was a three year old and by golly, I was not going to pass up ice cream. Fast forward through my half century on this earth and hand to God, I have never experienced a single bout of sore throat since that tonsillectomy at the age of three. I have had mind-blowing colds and knock down, drag out influenzas in my time, but not a twinge of pain in the throat ever. All because in the height of an emotional event a simple phrase that I would never have another sore throat was implanted in my mind. I wish the good doctor would have also told me I would be highly rich, attractive and wise, but that apparently was not spoken the night a three year old fell asleep afraid of the next day.

Thirty plus years after my body and mind-altering tonsillectomy, an amazing pediatric cardiothoracic surgeon took me aside in a peak of emotion and told me that the reconstruction of my son's heart had gone very well. He finished by saying that in a decade or so they would take a look at Jonathan and if he needed some work it would be taken care of. Those magic words implanted the belief that no matter what, Jonathan would always be all right, and intently placed me right into a "Normalcy Bias." From that point forward, I absolutely had every impression, belief, and surety that my child would survive and live a relatively normal life. Again, Jonathan himself, with his amazing and miraculous recoveries that astonished his cardiologists and surgeons, shored up the walls of my confidence. No matter what he faced, he always came out fine and therefore, always would be. Even in the final years when his collateral "cheaters" began to rob precious oxygen from his body, I knew in my mind that the doctors would fix the problem and his life would go on. They always had. Because of the Normalcy Bias I entered and lived within, I had every reason to be just like the majority of parents, expecting my little boy to outlive his father.

One of the driving desires in my journey towards healing after Jonathan passed was to determine if I was wrong, or even guilty in some way for existing in a world of denial. I truly wondered if I had actually caused my child harm by believing everything was always going to be status quo. Were there signs or symptoms I ignored along the way because of my belief nothing tragic would ever happen? Did I put my faith in doctors far too much? Did I fail to provide him all the medical care he needed for his fragile heart? The answer I found to those questions and more was no, of course, but I had to go down that road of discovery. I look back now on that sweet child's life, filled with the love, joy, and happiness he experienced. I am positive that the alternative of living in the gripping fear I might someday lose him would have actually retarded his incredible, albeit short, life. He had one filled with family and friends, as well as adventures, successes and failures. He had a comfortable life where he was not left wanting for much, emotionally or otherwise, and was loved unconditionally. In the very same manner, he certainly gave love and so much more back to everyone. Yet, before I could share my experiences with other grieving fathers, I also needed to know if I was alone in believing with all my heart that my son would always be around. My thirst for understanding turned back towards those dear children undergoing palliative care with an incurable illness. It is so very difficult to imagine what must go through the minds and hearts of parents who know in advance that they will experience the passing of their child. I cannot even bring myself to consider how the foreknowledge of Jonathan's passing would have been better or worse on me psychologically.

Sadly, I actually pondered this very question after the death of each of my parents. My mother passed away suddenly and without warning, which came as a painful shock, jolting my emotions and bringing on instant grief like a lightning strike. Less than a decade later my father, on the other hand, was diagnosed with an aggressive and incurable cancer that took him from a visibly strong and healthy man to a mere shell of his physical self in just a few short months. Soon he was surrounded by family and Hospice personnel and his passing was imminent. While the majority of shock came in the initial diagnosis, the amount of advanced time to process his loss before he was even gone was found to be no luxury at all. During the weeks leading up to his passing, I spent some very bittersweet time with him, as well as my brothers and sisters, and thought I had reluctantly come to an understanding and acceptance of the inevitable. Yet, the moment my father passed, the lightning strike of shock came regardless. Was I living in the normalcy bias even though told his passing loomed within just days? In the somewhat similar and heartbreaking experience of parents with terminally ill children, I found that even though surrounded with professional and compassionate support, the normalcy bias exists as well. When faced with the harsh and certain knowledge of their child's mortality, hope is still held out until the very end. For myself, I spent a great deal of time holding and begging my Jonathan to fight and come back to me long after the doctor told me he was gone. With every ounce of honesty in my own heart, I will say that I believed if I begged him hard enough, or if I just screamed at God for mercy, my son would snap out of it right there in my arms. Nevertheless, the lightning did strike.

I have spent a great deal of time discussing the role Normalcy Bias plays in a grieving father's life, regardless of whether the loss is unimaginably probable or tragically unexpected. Yet, I have not mentioned another aspect of normalcy bias which actually does come as a component of grieving, oftentimes immediately after the event. Wanting a normal activity, sometimes any normal activity is simply a coping mechanism as the mind attempts to register and sort out what took place. Much like a combat victim who loses a limb in battle and reports the lack of pain, our brain wants to mitigate the enormous emotional shock and instantaneous overload felt when faced with a loss. On the extreme side, this is the coping mechanism that finds the victim of a tornado, his house leveled to the ground, raking leaves in the front yard just as soon as the winds die down. It is the mental survival mode that causes the victim of an automobile accident to walk away from the scene and numbly head down a sidewalk as if nothing happened. I actually witnessed that often during my time as a police officer. The accident victim was not attempting to leave the scene of the crash, per se. Instead, the subconscious mind simply took control, cutting off the dreadful shock, and suggesting that a little stroll would be a lovely thing to do for just a little while as the mind sorts things out. That aspect of the normalcy bias is rarely long lasting or destructive, although it certainly could be if it disrupts everyday life or impedes the ability to take care of needs. Frankly, I recognize that I did experience this and was actually a bit glad it came about. After I left the hospital the morning my son passed, my logical brain told me to go straight to my church to begin arrangements, yet, my mind screamed constantly to get to my workbench. My workbench was my go to place and much like a child wanting to hide under the blankets during a thunderstorm, I wanted badly to get to any normal activity and just let things work themselves out on their own.

Any grieving father has a tendency to look back at the events that led up to a tragic loss and wonder about the past. Was there something undone that could have been a part of what happened, yet missed because we did not want to even imagine it? Like most men, I had every expectation that my child would live beyond my years and raised him with a deep longing to live life. Like most men, too, I should have no regrets for not preparing for an unpredictable disaster. Loving my dear son, Jonathan, and insuring he had an amazing and rewarding life while here with me was my normalcy bias. I was as prepared as I ever could be, which was actually not at all, and I am actually very much okay with that.

The Veil of Ego

"The ego relies on the familiar. It is reluctant to experience the unknown, which is the very essence of life."

— *Deepak Chopra*

As it always had, the hot water flowed from the shower head downward through my hair and over closed eyes, which allowed my mind to wander where it would. I was pretty numb that morning, knowing everything that could be done or should be done, had been done, and it was time to return to my job. I purposely tried to avoid the thoughts of my Jonathan's passing and desperately searched for something positive to occupy my conscious thoughts. Something normal to hold back the realization that just a few days earlier I would be wondering what he would be doing to pass a summer's day. I wandered back to thoughts of my own family. I honestly do not remember when or even if I was the one who reached out to tell my brothers and sisters that I had lost Jonathan, but just two days after, there they were walking up my driveway, having rallied together to cross half a continent to get to me. As I stood and watched, it seemed like Moses' leading his people out of Egypt, with my four brothers and sisters, nieces and nephews, their children and their children's children, boyfriends, girlfriends and long-time family friends converging on the house and spilling into the back yard. That was truly an amazing, bittersweet sight to see. While I thought nothing at the time could have brought light into my world, my heart certainly lifted and my will grew with the arrival of the Kelly clan and their undeniable devotion to family.

As I turned in the shower to let the hot water pound against the back of my neck, my memories turned to the funeral service when I sat down in the front row. After going over final touches with my pastor, Jonathan's casket was about to be wheeled in and placed in front of the church altar. That morning I felt sad, yet relieved that the casket lid was closed, which I had actually done myself just before visitation services the evening before. As I had seen more often than not, and was the case with Jonathan's remains, the morticians did not do a very good job. The face I saw before me did not look like my handsome young man. I was not terribly upset about that at the time, though, as I was resolved that Jonathan no longer occupied that body, as his innocent spirit had returned to God. Rather, I had thought of his young friends and schoolmates who would come to the viewing to say their goodbyes. I did not want their last memories to be an almost unrecognizable Jonathan. Instead, I closed the lid and focused everyone's attention to the dozens of wonderful pictures of my son placed throughout the viewing room. Regardless, sad or not, the closed casket was rolled into the church unceremoniously by men from the funeral home and I felt a little disappointed that people continued to mill about, and gave the casket no notice or reverence at all. Blame it on my past, but I believed in ceremony and respect, and was a tad annoyed that the church, so full of close family and friends, was still in "socializing" mode when the very body of my child had been brought in.

Someone who did notice Jonathan's casket was my "big" sister Debbie, who immediately took a seat directly behind me and placed a gentle, caring hand on my shoulder. Although I was hurting badly I was doing my best to hold it in. When I turned, I looked at my sister and immediately recognized the pain she had for me in her eyes. She surely loved Jonathan, of course. He was family to her. He was her nephew and a Kelly, and that alone was enough to be loved unconditionally. Nevertheless, being so far apart, she saw him maybe once or twice a year and I knew the hurt I saw was clearly for me alone. My incredible sister had become a second mom to me and my younger sibs long ago when our mother decided to take a job outside the house. Debbie is a tiny thing at around five feet in height and light enough to be afraid of strong winds, but she makes up for physical stature with the compassionate yet fierce heart of a lion tamer. I will not tell you of the traumas I inflicted on her as a bratty kid, but I will tell of later in life when I witnessed her corner one of her sons, a champion high school wrestler at the time, who had done something that obviously had not pleased her. There in her kitchen she stood on tippy-toes and went nose to nose with her son, his eyes saucer wide, and informed him in an Exorcist like voice, "You do that again and I will rip your face off." When she turned and walked away, I just looked at my poor nephew, smiled slightly, and told him "Gee, I have been there before." The smile, or smirk actually, was in homage to being the one who actually helped her hone those fine-parenting skills when I was in her care long before. Regardless, when I turned to my big sis at Jonathan's service and saw the obvious pain on her own face, in her eyes, I took her hand and attempted a charming grin, saying "Hey? It's not very fun here. Let's go somewhere else, huh?" Humor had always served me well in the past and it had seemed like a good way of easing some ache just then, but Debbie would not have any of it. She could see it in my own eyes and without hesitation suddenly climbed over the back of the seat row, even though we were right there at the end anyway, and sat down beside her little brother. We first touched foreheads, eyes closed and paused for just a few moments until I pulled back and put my arm around her shoulder. She then laid the side of her head against mine and we just sat quietly, as I allowed a few tears to fall. Debbie stayed there with me, quietly, mother like in her silent love, and I gratefully held on to her until the dreaded music began and my wife returned from socializing with others in attendance.

As the water temperature cooled a bit in my shower I realized I had been in there for some time, but cared little and adjusted the handle for more heat. My mind still wandered within the field of family and my thoughts turned to my older brother. Without reservation, Roger agreed to deliver the eulogy I had written for my son since there absolutely was no way I would be able. As it were, I had to write the piece in total privacy since I could barely formulate the thoughts in my head without tears, much less put them to paper. Roger had rightly taken his place as the family patriarch after our father passed several years ago and was the perfect choice to deliver my words of love and honor for my child. To describe him as a force of nature would be a huge undersell, as he has devoted his entire life to the battle of good versus evil, with a badge in his pocket and God in his heart. Having God in one's heart, however, comes with the wonderful and blessed price of actually having a heart. He made it somewhere into the second paragraph before his voice broke constantly from line to line and at one point he looked down from the podium with a glance that told me just how hard the reading was on him. His broken voice, however, added an honest compassionate tone that gave incredible honor and dignity to the words I had written from the depth of my own longing heart. My thoughts then turned to my younger sister, Karen, a force of nature in her own right, albeit it a whacky and wonderful force. Her love for family and for me has no equal, and she will go to great lengths to show you how much you love her too. Part wonderful goof ball and part mother to all, she has no issue walking into a room full of family in some funny hat or anything silly lying about to announce she is "everyone's" favorite. As I made another adjustment to the temperature in the shower, I could picture Karen during the days before and after the services. Each and every time I would walk into a room or anywhere within her view, she opened her arms widely and just stood there silently until I came to her and allowed myself to be wrapped inside her love.

Turning the hot water knob as far left as it would go, I realized my shower time would soon come to an end, just as being with my brothers and sisters had. I lingered, however, while I thought of the loving events over the past few days and my younger brother, Greg. I missed a lot of his life and sadly, some of the closest times we spent together over the years were when my mother and then my father passed away. During both horrible occasions, we would spend weeks together as a family and I would come to realize that Greg grew to be an incredible man who exudes love but humbly retains it behind a hint of reserved stoicism. He got that stoicism from Dad. While I can picture my father in the face of each brother and sister, I picture my father in Greg's spirit and mannerisms. There is no surprise there, as he had remained in close, almost day-to-day contact with our parents. He was the only child still at home when they escaped the suburbs of Washington, DC and bought the country store outside of Luray, Virginia. My sister Karen would spend a short time there as well, but would go off to live at college and only come home long enough to fill grocery bags with toilet paper and candy bars. As Greg aged, he married and settled inside the little town of Luray with his lovely wife, raised two beautiful daughters, and visited Mom and Dad often. To say he lived for them would do it no justice, as it was obvious that he intended to spend every minute he could with them. Our father was a man of few words, and if he liked you, he would give you the world. However, if he did not like you or you did him wrong, he would shut you right out of his life. No one wanted that, as Dad would give until he could give no more. That is Greg, as well. He took that from Dad and as I leaned on him during the funeral services, I felt my father with me in my kid brother, and knew if I asked him to, he would crawl over broken glass for me.

No matter how hard I turned the knob to the left, the hot water was spent and I had no choice but to shut the spray off. My Fortress of Solitude was closed for the day. I stepped from the shower, dried off and began to dress for work when it dawned on me that when I did leave for work I would enter a new life that was different than it had been just a few short days ago. All the things that had to be done which occupied my mind were completed and the fellowship and love I experienced in the company of such adoring siblings was now just a memory. I had to face reality, which included the fact that my Jonathan was gone from my life. With that wretched thought screaming to the very front of awareness I suddenly found myself standing at the foot of my bed, the palm of my hand rubbing the back of my neck, pondering a simply horrid question that would remain unresolved for a long time to come, "Who was I?"

I had no idea how that seemingly simple yet very complex question would ripple through every area of my being for a long time after I lost Jonathan. It had to be faced though, as he was gone and I was still here. While parts of me did not want to hear it, at some reasonable point in time, I had to return to a healthy and productive life. The alternative was absolutely not an option. I came to the awareness in my own spirit that the legacy my child left behind was not for me to wither away in disparity. It would take some time for me to come to an understanding, though, and I would look for answers only after I allowed myself to grieve. Unfortunately, for me it would not be a quick fix. I soon found that the journey towards healing must include addressing the three internal influences of self-worth, self-esteem, and ego. How did each affect me? First is self-worth. Without exception, anyone with a solid, loving childhood will have a foundational, positive sense of self-worth, molded through faith and an understanding that we do matter and are good in nature. Self-esteem, though similar, is a current belief in personal confidence and certainty in our abilities. While there are several differences, the simplest of the two is that self-esteem can ebb and flow with our current successes and failures while self-worth is always a part of who we are.

Then comes ego. I have learned to refer to that word by the acronym E.G.O, or "Edging God Out." Ego is living or acting in ways that you believe will bring respect or admiration from others, without looking inward at self-worth where the spirit of God lives inside us all. Ego is truly the false self and can easily, wrongfully erase and then take the place of self-esteem. While I firmly believe that ego can never eradicate a solid and fundamental self-worth, I know from experience that it can certainly hide it beneath a dark veil of clouds. I lived the majority of my life with low self-esteem and a false ego that dictated who I would be in front of others. Time after time, I would strive to be something I was not, just to create a persona of someone who was acceptable to others. It was not until the unspoken realization in my heart that one of the legacies left behind by my child was to unveil my self-worth from the dark clouds and live my life true to myself and to God.

Rediscovering my self-worth meant I also needed to understand the roadmap of my very own life. It was actually extremely difficult to go back over my past and consider each stage as if I were laying back on my own psychiatrist's couch. Yet, I did it, as far back as the mid 1960's in the Virginia suburbs outside of Washington, DC. I was around the young age of six then and blew up into a chubby little kid. I really have no idea why, since no one in my family was overweight, and truth be told I cannot remember a single friend or schoolmate who was overweight. Looking back at how active I was, the only down time in my daily kid life was Saturday morning cartoons. Other than that, I was part of a neighborhood full of kids who constantly enjoyed the stranger-danger free security that came as part of the suburbs back then. We ran freely in packs all day, every day and did not go home until our parents stood on the porch and screamed our names over and over. Big wheels, bikes, climbing trees and hide and seek were the staples. My weight during that time certainly made me different than those around me and I experienced the teasing you would imagine, with names such as fat-boy, jelly belly and such, but I had my core group of friends I had grown up with through school, cub scouts and little league sports. Even if I was overweight, I was part of the crowd in my school and in my neighborhood.

Just as I turned twelve, however, the family packed up and moved. I found myself entering a school system that included sixth graders in junior high school, instead of elementary. Since there were no other kids my age in my new neighborhood, I had to find my social life there only at school, where cliques were already established. Those who would be the upcoming sports stars had gone through the junior leagues together, and while I had played little league sports before, there was no way a new, chubby kid was going to fit in with the Middle School "jocks." If I wanted to fit in somewhere, I would have to turn to the other socio-established cliques of the times, made up of the geeks and the freaks, and I certainly was not going to be a geek. Whether I had the smarts for it was not the question. Those poor kids were teased to no end. I was already being teased for being heavy, so why bring additional insecurity into my life? That left the freaks, who eventually accepted me into the group and allowed me to belong somewhere.

By the age of fourteen or so when my body experienced the core dump of testosterone and acne, I shot up to six feet in height. Suddenly, as if overnight, not only did I slim down, I was actually bigger than most my age and my status with the freaks grew exponentially. For the next few years I hung out with the older kids in the crowd, which brought with it cars, booze and pot. Soon, sneaking out after everyone at home was asleep became the norm for me, as was skipping school, which caught up with me when I failed ninth grade for truancy. That was a big hit on me down deep inside and I knew something had to change. Thankfully, underneath the muck and mire of the false ego and low self-esteem, there was still the foundation of self-worth. Although I knew something had to change, however, I really made no effort to begin right off. My false ego was wrapped up in who I was to that gang of people I ran with, and until I found something else to transfer my ego to, I was going nowhere until it was right in front of my face.

God, however, got impatient and gave me a push early one summer morning. While on the drive to meet a buddy, I had agreed to stop by a townhouse to give a ride to his friend, a young lady I had never met. Her name was Stephanie and she wanted to join us for a day of swimming at the local pond. I agreed, and after knocking on the frame of an already open door, witnessed a strike of fate. There before my eyes this stunning beauty, the girl of my unknown dreams, walked down a flight of stairs and directly towards me. Our eyes met and never parted as she neared, and as corny as it sounds, and as her mother witnessed, we fell in love right there on her front porch. We became inseparable and I no longer wanted to keep my ego in the hands of a gang of friends going nowhere. I placed them right in Stephanie's hands the day we met and my desires to be a better kid were soon transcended by a desire to become a better man, because I knew I was going to marry that girl of my dreams one day. With a new direction, most of the bad elements within my group of friends were whittled away. My time for extracurricular fun was also taken up while I worked at my father's service station in order to have plenty of gas and money to take my baby out. As for school, my attendance and grades improved quickly and I actually found myself with enough credits to catch back up with my original class, not only graduating on time, but on the school's Honor Roll, as well.

I began to feel a great deal of self-esteem with what I had done. I had been such a poor kid in my teens, with a runaround lifestyle full of booze, drugs, and a bad crowd. Then, I felt as if I had turned my life around, and just like my older brother and sister, was on my way to earning my parent's pride. After I graduated, a full time job and an apartment were next, along with an engagement ring, since I immediately asked the girl of my dreams to marry me. When she said yes, I knew I would be a reputable man before my parents, as I would have a great wife, a good job and eventually a house and kids. Throughout that shady past, I had pulled away when I felt I had let my parents down, and avoided home and family. I wanted back in, though. I would no longer be the chubby kid, or the bad kid or the kid who failed a grade in school. I would be a man with an intact self-esteem who would allow his parents to hold their heads high. If only life were that easy, though. Stephanie actually moved into the apartment with me before the wedding when her parents moved south to Florida. It had been in their plans for some time and when her father retired, the move followed immediately. Living together was frowned on in those days, but she and I did not really care, as we had no desire to be separated by a thousand miles until we wed. Actually, I did not have the confidence nor clear view of my own self-esteem to take a chance on letting Stephanie out of my grasp. Yet, living together for any young couple is difficult, married or not, and when mixed with immaturity it can be fatal. A silly argument found her heading to Florida for a cool off period and my bruised ego said and did things to turn her sojourn into a so long. I was alone and unsure of who I was again. Sure, I loved Stephanie but had to handle the false ego hit that I had not lived up to everything she needed in a man. Also heavy on my mind at the time was also the fact that my designs on becoming what I thought to be acceptable within the family faded away too. Without a wife, who would I be?

It would have been nice if shattering an ego would have led me back to the foundation of self-esteem, but youth and a desire for that acceptance with someone, anyone, quickly won the fight, and I turned back to the old group of friends. The good times not only rolled again, they soon took over as they will with someone of low self-esteem who must seek acceptance from others. Thankfully, dignity, which is a spark of self-worth, fired from deep inside of my soul one morning as I sat despondently with my face down in the palm of my hands. I had quit my well-paying job when it got in the way of my lifestyle and rented a room at a friend's house. Night after night I was awakened constantly by the never ending flow of drunken or stoned strangers outside my door. That was the case that very night as well, and I could take it no longer. Sure, I was despondent but what would I do? My chase for a false ego had led me right to where I was that morning and I just needed to head in a direction that would make my life respectable and acceptable. What direction would I head, however? I then thought of my father who had enlisted in the Air Force during the Korean War, escaped the coalmines of the Appalachian Mountains, and picked up a trade as a mechanic. What he became put a roof over the head of his wife and five kids, and he was very well respected. I wanted that. I also thought of my older brother Roger, who had enlisted in the Corps, married his own high school sweetheart, and started a successful life as a cop after he honorably discharged. I wanted that as well, and by golly, the service would be the path for me.

I dressed and drove to the Marine Corp recruitment office that very morning and not only enlisted, but selected Military Police as my MOS, or Military Occupation Specialty. While it seemed to family members that I followed in the footsteps of my big brother by becoming a Jarhead and a cop, that was not it at all. Back during high school, I met with military recruiters and although I had no desire to enlist at the time, knew the ins and outs of each branch of the service. If I was going to make a wholesale change to my life, it absolutely had to be through baptism by fire. During the drive to the enlistment office, I fully convinced myself that the Marine Corps would either make me or break me. I would not end up back with my face in my hands. As for selecting law enforcement, I would be lying if I did not say my brother was and remains a strong mentor in my life, and following in his footsteps would always be wise. Yet, my reasoning was not that, at all. Instead, I thought only that if I were going to turn my life around, it had to be the complete polar opposite of the very lifestyle that led me to the question, "Who am I?" I would find another ego, it would be huge, and I would have respect.

I survived the mental and physical torture that was Marine Corps Boot Camp, Parris Island, South Carolina and graduated with a month's leave before reporting to MP training. I deliberately found my way back to the old stomping grounds, and hoped to somehow find Stephanie there. My heart told me that although it was highly improbably, it was still possible. I knew she had a sister who still lived somewhere in the area and maybe, just maybe Stephanie got homesick. If only I could find her, I would show her I could be the man who could live up to her love and respect. Maybe I still had a shot to marry my high school sweetheart and start a family with a good career in the military. It would not be, however. Almost immediately, I ran across Amy, her best friend, and listened sadly as she told me of how Stephanie was still in Florida, in a long-term relationship with a boyfriend and heavily into the church lifestyle. Maybe it was my own guilt for my past, but hearing she was heavily involved with the church told me she had no intent on returning to Virginia at all. I left for Military Police training disappointed and would go on to serve my four-year stint in the Corps, returned to Northern Virginia and joined my brother on the local police department.

Along the way in both the military and the police department, I would go through a number of failed relationships, each time trying to find someone to hold onto my ego and give me that family life which I thought I was supposed to have. Yet, each failure would take me farther and farther away from those family members who loved me unconditionally. As it had in the past, visits with my parents and participation in family outings became few and far between, and I began to build my false ego only for me. While I could write some very racy books on myself as a cop, suffice it to say my off duty hours began to take on an irresponsible life almost as destructive as my early teen years. Nothing I did was illegal, of course, but a social life became my driving force as I took advantage of the ego of being a cop and a former Marine. Living a destructive life can be exhaustive, thankfully, and it was not long before that life built around wine, women and song thankfully took its toll. After almost a decade on the department God had enough and shut down my freewheeling social life when I met Marki, my wife, and we fell in love over coffee.

Life would change fast after that, and in what seemed like the snap of a finger I left the police department for a job in the private sector, married Marki and would become the proud father of Jonathan. Because Jonathan's reconstructive surgeries on his heart would require extensive hospital stays, followed by at-home care, a Monday through Friday day job was a blessing. I would visit my parents more often and gladly come to family gatherings, where I felt I finally fit in. I did not really have the home yet, but it did not matter. We left our apartment and moved in with her parents so Jonathan could have the extensive love and homecare he needed as he went through the first few years of his life. Since his back-to-back surgeries would take place a short distance from my in-law's home, it just seemed practical at the time and we moved in together. After those few years, however, practicality turned to love of Jonathan and since his grandparents had become another mother and father to him, we mutually decided to stay together and moved to a larger home in Mississippi. While they would purchase the new home, I would take over financial responsibility for the bills, home repair, and maintenance, with the idea that the home would be ours when the grandparents passed. Thus, I would not really have the home part of my life yet, but I had the wife and the child, and with the adoration I had for my son, my life was complete enough.

Throughout Jonathan's life, I held some very prestigious positions with large defense contractors in the security field, yet I never looked to them for ego or self-esteem. The good pay and executive titles only served as a means to support my child and provide him with the best health insurance available. As Jonathan grew, my ego actually became wrapped around being the father to that miracle child. I was the dad to someone who defied death as a newborn and mystified the doctors over the years with his strength, determination, and an almost indescribable will to live. Friends, other parents, and schoolteachers, as well as almost anyone who met Jonathan fell in love with him for his story, his personality, and his resolve. Unfortunately, my ego soon thought that included me. I was the proud father who had played a large role in Jonathan's development, and soon I felt as if just being that father was my sole purpose on earth. It would seem that with my ego occupied by such a noble cause, my self-esteem would have good reason to be confident and strong in who I was. I had the wonderful child, shared a marvelous joint home with Jonathan's grandparents, and had a wife.

Regrettably, Jonathan and I lost his mother to an emotional condition when he was around the age of eight. Remaining respectful to her, I will just say Marki was always a loving mother to Jonathan, and he loved and doted on her constantly until the day he passed. Her condition, however, involves a lack of an attention span that hinders her ability to perform many of the daily functions of being a parent. It is also accompanied by what health professionals term as a "Lack of Awareness," meaning that to herself, there is nothing wrong and our encouragements for treatment throughout the years were always refused. She remains a very happy soul, however, and of no danger to herself or others, so she cannot be forced against her will to seek help. As I studied her condition over the years, I was not surprised to find she is not alone, as many similar to her will live out their lives the way they are. As far as being a wife, I fell in love with her, married her and she is still with me. She was, and remains the mother of my child and I would never let anything bad happen to her. Regardless, my ego and self-esteem were completely in the hands of Jonathan. I had served honorably as a Marine and cop, but that was behind me. I held big roles in large corporations, too, but there was no service to that. I was not really giving to anyone other than Jonathan, as my true motivation was to make sure I brought home a nice paycheck. I had a wife, but not a partner, and lived in a nice home but not a true owner. Even with all that, I was still Jonathan's father, the most important label I could ever ask for. On June 13, 2013, however, not only did I lose my son, but also I lost myself. While it seems almost callous to say, along with my son went my self-esteem and the ego I placed in his care. The morning after the funeral services were over and my family had returned home, I left the shower, stood at the foot of my bed and once again had to ask, who am I?

It would not be until another morning in the shower, several months later, that I would begin grieving his loss and look for the true answer of who I really was. I came to realize that with all the things Jonathan had left me, one of his greatest legacies was giving me a glimpse of my self-worth. That morning as I collapsed to my knees on the shower floor, I thought back to something I had said over a telephone conversation with my boss just the day after Jonathan had passed. After we had spoken for a few moments about life insurance and taking all the time I needed, I surprisingly uttered in a broken voice, "This is going to change me. There is no way it won't. Please help me make sure it doesn't change me in the wrong way." The moment I said those words I had no idea where they came from as they left my mouth. My brain had not even formulated the thoughts in advance and they just seemed to come from somewhere deep inside me. On that shower floor, however, I accepted that my self-worth was really just trying to speak up for itself that day, as it was wise and knew me very well. It was absolutely sure I would attempt to seek a false ego to regain my self-esteem, and before the shower, I did just that.

Without a wife to turn to at home, I turned to others and with online social media coming of age, it was easy to stay connected. There were those who had truly cared for me and others who only wanted to make me feel better after my loss, but the reason mattered not to me. I would use all of their words to feed my ego and when I could not reach out instantly for my fill, I would seek them out with almost fanatical uproar and a passionate need to hear what a good guy I was. I also actively began to seek out admiration at work where I had always led others by example, and instead annoyed coworkers with peacock like displays of my abilities in hopes they would openly admire me. At home, I avoided contact with those in the house as they were still in mourning and of no use to my ego building. Instead, I hid myself at the workbench where I identified myself as a woodworker and displayed my crafts on the internet for anyone with a computer to see, and waited to be patted on the back for my talents. There was so much more I could list but it was easy to see I was desperately in need of an ego. I had to be somebody.

All of my desires to be something to someone were destructive to both myself and to others. I am sure now that if they had continued for too much longer would have resulted in something very bad. I would stop, thank goodness, and understand just who I really am the fateful day when Jonathan returned to my heart and I grieved his loss. Of course, when he passed, a piece of me went with him, but he let me know that morning when the grief came that underneath it all is self-worth. It is the knowledge I have in being a morally good and just person, and above all else, a creation and child of God. I suddenly knew that with the compassion of God, the ego was no longer needed, and without the cloud of ego, the self-esteem cannot help but grow strong. The building self-esteem would allow me to see that while Jonathan was here, he brought out so much in me, as together we witnessed and discovered humility, compassion for family and friends, as well as the pure beauty of life itself. Those words were so foreign to me before he was born. After he let me recall who I was, I would look even deeper inside than I had when he was here. Through that, I would come to understand that all of my life I had an amazing family that wanted nothing more than to give me unconditional love. I also understood that beyond any measure of others, I am worthy of living a healthy, productive and enjoyable life even when no one but God will hold my hand. Who was I to experience, take joy and love throughout Jonathan's time with me, and just throw it all away because he was called home? The true legacy he left for me was to reveal that, without question, my self-worth was given to me through the spirit of God who dwells within us all and it can always be relied upon as the very foundation of who I truly am. If I would always recognize that very fact, my need for acceptance by others would never Edge God Out, as the ego would be too weak to hide my self-worth under a veil of deception.

I will admit that the destruction and eventual redevelopment of my self-worth, self-esteem and the need to let go of the false ego are far more extreme than others. Maybe not. I was not the best kid. Possibly that is not even a consideration in many other fathers who have lost a child. Yet, if only one other grieving father can benefit from my egotistical journey of sorts, than I am honored to have served. I do have an admission, however. I would like to disclose that I still have an ego, albeit one that does not control my life as much. I am a man, after all, and to say I would ignore anyone who gave me praise or admiration would simply be untrue. Like many other aspects of my life I would like to conquer, I will keep trying. I imagine if I succeed, I can be found atop a mountain, wearing only an orange robe while I contemplate the spirit of man. For now, it is simply enough to recognize when ego pops into my mind, and it will, I should only recognize it as not positive or self-worthy, and then dismiss it. A wise man once said, even in the best of good people, there will always be a small person inside who wants to be bad. It would be silly to fight with that little person, as it solves nothing…and fighting with yourself just looks silly in public.

The Return to Faith

"Faith is taking the first step even when you don't see the whole staircase."

~ Martin Luther King Jr.

It was nine-thirty in the morning and people milled to and fro within the cafeteria of Fairfax Hospital, itself found hauntingly deep within the bowels of the facility. I was told earlier by Shelly, Doctor Akl's Physician's Assistant, that the surgery on my infant son Jonathan would take several hours and I should find the cafeteria and eat something. There was no way I could eat, but a cup of coffee would be welcome. I was exhausted, having not been able to sleep at all throughout the night. I woke at four in the morning, traveled to the hospital, and surrendered my beautiful newborn baby Jonathan to the surgical team. As I held him in my arms throughout the pre-op procedures, he never once cried. Yet, I would try to make him smile with my high-pitched gitchie-goo noises while I tickled his tiny chest, cooed in his ear, and touched his button nose. On one occasion, I traced the tip of my index finger from his little pinkish nose down to his closed lips, which instinctively opened and clamped tightly around my finger. He closed his sweet eyes and suckled for just a moment before I slowly pulled my finger from his mouth with some guilt in the awareness of how hungry he must have been. Under doctor's orders, Jonathan was not fed for twelve hours before the surgery and as I pulled my finger from his wanting mouth I expected backlash for my tease. There was none, save for a bit of frustrated bike pedaling of his wee legs and some waving about of his fisted hands, which soon slowed as his eyes clinched tightly and his open mouth was overtaken with a deep, adorable and lengthy yawn. I moved my face closer to his and took one of his little fists in my own hand as the yawn ended and he slowly opened and closed his mouth a few times, tenderly smacking his lips as if he expected to taste formula. When none was discovered, Jonathan opened his sweet blue eyes, looked straight into mine, and smiled a big toothless smile.

Many have claimed that infants do not smile, and anything that might give the appearance of one must only be the result of gas or involuntary muscle movements. Forget all that. It had been a smile, all right. My eyes were locked with his and I felt it. I felt a connection and a love for this little person like I had never felt love before. I felt really, really traitorous at that moment as well. My gosh! I was that child's father and long before he was born, I had already acknowledged that I was to be his protector and it would be my lifelong responsibility to ensure his safety and security. Yet there in the pre-op room I was about to voluntarily hand over this happy, innocent child to a procedure, the very danger of which could take his life, where he would have his precious chest ripped wide open and his fragile heart assaulted. As I looked directly down into my son's eyes, I realized he had no idea what

I was about to allow happen to him. It took a phenomenal amount of resolve not to turn and run in a last ditch effort to take my swaddling bundle of beautiful boy and slip quietly off to some place far away and safe from the outside world. I did not, though, and within a few minutes, Shelly arrived and had me "gown up" so that I could carry Jonathan back to the operating room where I gently laid him down onto a warmed blanket that covered the operating table. I leaned down on my elbows where my nose could nuzzle gently around his ear while I whispered, "You Are Daddy's brave boy. I love you, buddy and I'll be right here when you wake up."

I probably repeated those whispers a dozen times before the anesthesiologist announced he was ready to administer the gas. I backed my face away only slightly while the small plastic mask was placed over Jonathan's mouth and nose. I watched his tiny eyes as they looked one way and then the other a few times before he found my gaze just as his eyelids closed slowly. When they did, I felt a pain inside my soul I had never felt before. That familiar feeling also came to my forehead as tears welled and then freely cascaded down and became absorbed in the surgical mask on my face. I felt love like I had never felt before and every instinct inside told me I did not want to walk away from my baby. I turned to Shelly and saw that her eyes, the only features of her face not hidden behind her own mask, were wet as well, and I silently spoke to her. With just the squint of my watery eyes, she heard my unspoken plea and quietly whispered back in response, "Yes. It's fine. Give him a kiss." With that, I pulled down my own mask to just below my lips, felt the dampness from the tears wipe down across my exposed cheeks and leaned forward to kiss my baby softly. "Daddy loves you. I will be right here when you wake up."

As I walked by Shelly towards the door, she placed a caring hand on my shoulder and instructed me to head for the cafeteria and maybe get something to eat. She also reminded me the surgery would take several hours and she would call my cell phone from time to time with updates. With that, I left my precious son behind with kind but relative strangers and made my way to the hospital eatery, grabbed a cup of coffee and took a seat. I had nothing else to do but sit, worry and pray. Pray? I felt a strong need to and wanted to, but would God even want to hear my prayers, though? I had not done a whole lot of praying in my life and I was concerned the big guy might take an exception to me. Besides, I had never led my own formal prayer before. Was I to pray aloud in front of everyone in the room or could I just think it quietly in my mind? I never got the opportunity to figure it out that morning since during my little spiritual conundrum I noticed a familiar face had entered the cafeteria. It was Pastor Ralph. The good pastor was not only the man who had been my wife's minister throughout her entire life and performed our wedding, but was the very same man who found us upstairs in the lobby of the very same hospital a few weeks back and led us in prayer. The significance of the man's appearance in the cafeteria that morning was reverent enough, yet went so much deeper for me as I began to see God at work in my life.

To explain my divine awe that morning in the hospital cafeteria I must go back to Jonathan's birth, which actually took place across town. I wanted my son to be born in Alexandria Hospital because I had been born there so many years before and thought it would be something he and I could always share. The birth was complicated enough, as my wife remained in labor for many, many painful hours before someone finally realized her innards were not suited to allow such a large child, at almost ten pounds, to simply pop right out. Therefore, a Caesarian Section was eventually performed and while she and the baby remained in recovery through the following day, the horrible discovery of his failing heart was made. During swift consultations with the doctors on staff, I was told my son's heart was in great distress and he might not make it through the night. I was given the option of remaining there where they could do whatever they could, or have the child transferred to Children's Hospital in Washington, DC. Knowing the renown of such a great medical facility for kids, I opted immediately to have him sent there. Jonathan was transported quickly by ambulance and before I even parked my car and got inside, a team of pediatric cardiologists had already surrounded him and diagnosed his condition. He had been born with Hypo-plastic Left Heart Syndrome, which meant the left side of his heart had not grown in his mother's womb. Without immediate intervention of some sort, he would not survive for more than another few days at best.

Within an hour of my arrival at Children's Hospital, I was introduced to Doctor Carol Cook, who would serve as the lead surgeon on Jonathan's case. For some internal but unknown reason I liked her right away. I reasoned at the time it was the way she compassionately took me from doom and despair to immediate hope. In no hurry whatsoever, she clarified exactly what a Hypoplastic Left Heart was and went into great detail as she described the multiple open-heart procedures that would have to be performed to save my baby boy. Understandably, she threw words at me that meant little until that day, such as the Norwood procedure, followed by the Glen, and when he was old and strong enough, the final Fontan procedure. If all went well, by the age of three or so Jonathan would have a fully functional right side to his heart, which would allow him to live a relatively normal life. The good doctor went on to explain they would determine the correct medications to stabilize Jonathan for the time being, as he would need to strengthen up a bit before the first surgery at around three months of age. Up to that point, I had assumed the surgeries would begin right away, but when I heard we would wait for three months I wondered what the living arrangements would be while we waited, as I had no intent of leaving my child alone. I was extremely relieved, however, when Doctor Cook said I would be taking Jonathan home once they had him stabilized, and except for daily medications, he would be treated, and loved and cuddled as any newborn baby would. I was relieved all right, but I was also incredibly scared. I would not only be a father, but a medical caregiver as well.

The combinations of various medications were adjusted to stabilize Jonathan for his interim stay at home, and before I knew it, Doctor Cook gave the final marching orders for care. There actually was not much, really. Other than administering his prescribed meds precisely as directed, the only caution mentioned by the doctor was about any fever Jonathan might develop. She sternly advised that if Jonathan were to spike any temperature over one-hundred and three degrees he must be taken immediately to the closest emergency room. Easy enough, I thought. I could certainly do that if needed. With that in mind, Jonathan was taken home and for several weeks, I would be overwhelmed in the joys of fatherhood, almost forgetting about what loomed ahead for that innocent boy. He was everything expected from an infant and more. He cried little, ate well, and was a cuddly little buddy to fall asleep on the couch with. He was the center of attention and I was a proud father. Late one afternoon, however, the fever came. When it hit one-hundred and three degrees, Jonathan was quickly bundled and rushed to Fairfax Hospital, only fifteen minutes away, where my anxiety level rose immediately. Not only did it initially seem to take far too long for a doctor to examine my child, but also when the order came for admittance, it seemed forever before a pediatric room would become available. Once there, more delay came as the doctors awaited consultations with the pediatric staff at Children's Hospital, and finally the order was made to simply give the child some fever reducer and observe him overnight.

It was almost ten at night before Jonathan received the medication meant to reduce his fever, which had climbed to one-hundred and six degrees by then. The hallways had become empty and dark, with the lights dimmed and a noticeable reduction of staff about. His fever not only refused to subside, but actually climbed to one-hundred and eight degrees by three in the morning. Apart from the young, female nurse who would come by every fifteen minutes or so, Jonathan received no attention from an actual doctor. On what would be the nurse's final visit, my anxiety turned to anger and fear as I irately asked her why I had not seen the doctor I demanded on both her previous checks. She apologized and reported that the doctor had been notified and was with another child in distress but would be with me shortly. As she left the room I turned and witnessed my father-in-law, who had joined me earlier when I sent my wife home to rest, as he ran cold water over washcloths and then wrapped them around the body of my child in hopes it would bring the fever down. That was enough for me and I walked into the hallway and screamed for a doctor at the top of my lungs. I knew other children were asleep at the time but I honestly felt I had no other choice. I knew my own child was lying in the room behind me fighting for his very life and no one would help. I continued my yells for a doctor and after several minutes, the large double doors to my left burst open and I witnessed a group of about six individuals that ran towards me. Backlit by lights beyond the double doors, I imagined them to be security, but I did not care. Jonathan would get attention.

As the group neared, I expected to be manhandled and shoved back into my son's room but instead I was ignored, as a number of men in scrubs brushed by me quickly and entered the room. Inside they unhooked monitors and wires, and quickly pointed Jonathan's hospital crib towards the door. As they pushed through the doorway, one of the group stopped and instructed me to grab any personal effects and follow, as Jonathan was being taken to the NICU, or Neo-Natal Intensive Care Unit. After a series of hallways and elevators were navigated, we entered the NICU and Jonathan's crib was swarmed by doctors, nurses and Lord knows who else. For quite some time he was tended to by many on the staff and at some point, I was told his little heart had gone into almost complete failure. Also, I discovered it was not my hallway screaming that brought the rescue team running after all. Rather, it had been the attending doctor in the pediatric wing who ordered the transfer when he heard the fever had hit so high. Yet, I still felt justified in my hallway tirade, somehow. Regardless, at around eight in the morning Jonathan's mother joined me just as a fresh group of doctors surrounded Jonathan's crib. One of the doctors, a NICU "Intensivist" we would get to know very well, advised us to take a break and go for a walk or something for an hour or so. Jonathan was stable for the time being but the team of doctors wanted to examine him closer and when we came back, he would give us a better idea of what had happened and what would happen.

Despondently, my wife and I made our way through the hallways to the main lobby of the hospital where we found a couple of comfortable chairs to sit back in and wring our hands. As I filled her in on the events of the night, I was startled as she abruptly shouted out, "Pastor Ralph." She had spotted the pastor as he entered the lobby and turned immediately towards us as he recognized the caller of his name. We all sat for several minutes and my wife and I not only told him of the recent happenings, but also shamefully had to apologize that we had not even informed him earlier of Jonathan's birth. Of course, we would blame it on having been busy with the hospital stays, special childcare needs and whatever else we could use to redeem ourselves, and the pastor would accept it all with a non-condescending face. I was sure he had heard many excuses for being left out of the loop in his day.

Regardless, my wife and I had come to the assumption that the pastor had arrived that morning specifically to see us. Surely, someone had told him that morning and he came to comfort my wife, whom he had baptized as a baby and married as a woman. He had not, however. He had come to the hospital to visit another church member and had no knowledge we were there. Pastor would spend about twenty minutes with us that morning, doing what he did best by explaining how God works in mysterious and wonderful ways before he announced he needed to get on with his visit and his day. Before he left, however, he asked us to join him in prayer for Jonathan's health and we joined hands, bowed our heads, and he began.

As Pastor Ralph began to pray for Jonathan I immediately noticed I was not embarrassed to be openly involved in prayer within a busy hospital lobby, where people walked only feet away. For me, any past prayer had been largely relegated to inside of a church on my infrequent visits, and maybe during Christmas and Thanksgiving dinners at home. I had never prayed or even been led in prayer in public before, but it just felt right that morning. During the pastor's prayers, however, I took notice when not just once or twice but several times throughout his lengthy pleas, he would repeat his request for God to ensure that Jonathan was in the right hands. "Only the right hands could heal him, God," he would repeat over and over again, with noticeably heightened passion on each repetition. For myself, each time he asked for the right hands I reacted strangely inside and felt flush and warm, as I hung on the words and silently spoke them in response after they came from his mouth. When Pastor finished his prayer and promised to visit Jonathan when allowed, we exchanged handshakes and hugs, and walked back to the NICU to be at our son's side. We had not been gone long enough, however, as I noticed the huddle that still surrounded our child's crib. The Intensivist noticed us though, and broke away long enough to let us know that our baby was doing much better and had stabilized well. He also disclosed that the doctors at Children's Hospital had arranged to expedite Jonathan's first open heart surgery in light of the recent heart failure, but he would remain in their NICU at Fairfax for at least a few days of observation. After his kind briefing the Intensivist returned to the gang around Jonathan as I spied a small waiting room just about twenty yards from the action. The room was empty and quiet so I would find a comfortable seat and took comfort in the news that Jonathan had stabilized and was out of immediate danger.

The morning dragged on, and I stood like a guard at Jonathan's crib when I could and moved off to the waiting room when I got in the way of the staff's attentions. Day turned to night and night into morning as sleep would come in twenty or thirty-minute bouts either crib side in a small recliner or in one of the semi-comfy chairs in the waiting room. It was during one of those brief sojourns in the waiting room that I noticed Dr. Carol Cook, Jonathan's lead surgeon from Children's Hospital. Through the glass panes that served as the wall, I watched as the doctor walked right by without a glance in our direction, which caused my wife and me to jump out into the hallway and mug her in appreciation. How kind was it, after all, for her to come all the way to Fairfax Hospital and check on our child? We were surprised, however, when the doctor confessed to having no idea Jonathan was even there. Nor had she any indications he was even in distress. With earnest sympathy, she said she would go see Jonathan immediately but surprised us even further by telling us she no longer worked for Children's Hospital. While we listened, stunned and a little concerned at first, she detailed how just the very day before she unexpectedly received a career-changing offer to take a position there at Fairfax Hospital on the team of a top rated child heart surgeon named Doctor Bechara Akl. The surgeon had been consistently ranked within the top three pediatric cardiothoracic surgeons in the country over the past decade, and he practiced right there at little ole' Fairfax Hospital.

I knew in my very soul that day what would come next was a direct result of God's intervention. Doctor Cook asked if we wanted to have Doctor Akl perform Jonathan's procedures. Was she kidding? Of course, I wanted someone so highly ranked and obviously revered to work on my boy. My response was an immediate yes. Truth be told, I secretly felt a little embarrassed and naive that I had not known or even considered a ranking system for heart surgeons. Moreover, and certainly not taking anything away from Doctor Cook, what kind of putz father was I for not even considering her rankings, ratings or whatever when she was assigned to Jonathan? She had landed at Children's Hospital, however, so she must have been good as well. Regardless, the doctor further informed us she had already mentioned Jonathan to Doctor Akl the day before while she shared with him the cases she would leave behind at Children's Hospital. When she told him of Jonathan's condition, Doctor Akl commented on how he would have liked Jonathan to be his patient since he would be the perfect candidate for the relatively new procedures he used.

I felt a bit of ease when I learned that a top ranked surgeon felt my son was a perfect candidate. To me, that said he should do just fine. After hearing all of those words from Doctor Cook, I had already begun to feel divine intervention in play, but if I had any hesitation or doubt, they were soon put aside as the doctor said her goodbyes. As we exchanged pleasantries, she stated she may not actually see us for some time, as she would still be finishing up with some patients at Children's, but she would call the doctor right away and the arrangement would be put in place. She finished by saying, "You will be a lot better off here. Dr. Akl is the right hands for Jonathan." She said the right hands! I heard her. Those were the very words repeated so many times in Pastor Ralph's prayers only the day before when he popped up without being called. Pastor had prayed and led prayer asking for God's favor in placing Jonathan in the right hands. God, in his grace, moved mountains so that the very next day my son was in the hands of one of the best in the country. Over the next few days, without the knowledge of the metrics or magic that took place in the back offices of the two hospitals, Jonathan had become a patient of Doctor Akl, and would remain in the NICU for another week. I would be informed through Doctor Akl's team that Jonathan had stabilized much better than expected. Because of this, the doctor delayed the first surgery by thirty days, which allowed Jonathan to gain some strength before the first very invasive surgery. Jonathan was allowed to come home once again, where I watched diligently for fever and cursed the calendar as the days flew by.

On the morning of that thirtieth day, I gently but so reluctantly surrendered my child to the warm operating table, knowing soon his entire body would be under duress while horrendous but life-saving changes would be made to his tiny heart. After I received the silent approval of Shelly to kiss Jonathan's rosy cheek, I made my way to the hospital cafeteria for a cup of coffee, plenty of worry and a prayer, if I could figure out how to do it. That was when Pastor Ralph once again walked in unexpectedly. I looked to my wife partially in surprise but also had to ask if she had thought to let the church know about Jonathan. She had not, and we approached and greeted the pastor a little more timidly than we had just a few short weeks earlier. Expectedly, he had not come because of Jonathan. Once again, the Pastor was there to visit another church member. Regardless, I wasted no time as I regaled him with the miraculous outcome of his previous prayer. I thought it would have been retorted with the comment, "And still I don't see you on Sundays," but that did not come. Instead, Pastor Ralph maintained his typical non-condemnatory posture and offered to lead us in prayer once again.

Jonathan's first open-heart surgery went well but he still had the difficult recovery to go through. For weeks afterwards, he would remain in the NICU under the caring hands of the doctors and nurses there, as well as Pastor Ralph, who would visit and pray regularly. When Jonathan had recovered beyond the expectations of his doctors and was sent home, I would leave the hospital with a stronger belief in

God, yet took no time or effort to take it further. I had been raised with a belief that God was there and I was amazed in the grace He had given me, but I had the excuse of work and special childcare issues that took up my time. Jonathan had two more open-heart surgeries to come, after all. Because of that, he was relegated to the house in order to avoid viruses and other nasty things that could attack his weakened immune system. Taking him even to Sunday service at church, with all those people about, was certainly out of the question. It mattered little to the patient pastor, though, as he continued to work through God for us.

Jonathan would be admitted for his second procedure and while the operation went relatively well, Jonathan's little body had a great deal of trouble dealing with the punishing effects of another open-heart surgery. With as much compassion as possible, I suppose, Shelly had to break the terrible warning that there was a very good chance Jonathan might not survive. He hung in there, though and as the days went by, Easter Morning came. His mother and I, along with her parents, were joined by other family members who had stopped in. They had attended their own Easter Services and afterwards came by to check on my son, who must have been a shock to them while he laid asleep in a medical coma. He was being kept alive only by the life support of a breathing tube, external pacemaker, and what seemed to be miles of medical tape and vital stat wires. I could tell by the look in the eyes of those in the room that each silently wondered if that precious child would be with us much longer. While the room remained somber and family members took turns cycling to Jonathan's crib side to stroke a tiny hand and whisper secret wishes, the door to the room opened and Pastor Ralph quietly stepped inside. There he was again.

As before, we had failed to let the pastor know of Jonathan's surgery, yet when asked how he knew, his answer was a little more logical, but still amazing. Once again, he had come to check on a church member and stated that God mentioned he might stop by the information booth to ask if Jonathan was a patient. Of course, he was not in the least surprised when he found out Jonathan actually was. While not everyone understood the level of awe and humor as I, it stirred a light laugh around the room. Then, the pastor astounded me further by asking if he could baptize both Jonathan and me that morning, and said he could think of no better time than Easter to do so. I knew so little of religion at the time, aware only that I had attended Sunday School at a Southern Baptist Church as a child and stopped that when I was old enough to join the congregation upstairs for services. The pastor and his church were Lutheran and although he had married my wife and me, I was not a member. Yet, over the last year or so, I had witnessed enough through the power of prayer and I was sold. Therefore, in that NICU recovery room, with Jonathan clinging to his very life, Pastor performed the Baptism rites on my son and me in front of family and friends. Afterwards he led all in a simple prayer, asking God to see to Jonathan's swift recovery and departed with the promise to visit often. At nearly seven o'clock that Easter evening, Jonathan began to fight and gag around his breathing tube. By midnight, it was removed so he could breathe on his own and the next day he was brought out of his medical coma. Jonathan not only recovered quickly, but once again did so beyond the expectation of his doctors. His heart was beating well, his blood was flowing just fine, and we were joyfully sent home.

The third and final surgery came and went, with the same anxieties, risks, and fears as the first two, except by that time we had kept Pastor Ralph in the loop. He visited often during recovery, led us all in prayer, and before I knew it, Jonathan was back at home. He had defied the warnings and cautions and although he would experience minor issues throughout his young life, he would thrive and grow wonderfully. One would think with the miracles I had witnessed through prayer that I would have been fanatically driven to dive so much deeper into our Lord and Savior. At the time I rationalized that the only way to know Him better was through the church. There would have to be organized religion and a man of the cloth to guide me, and while I felt my life was far too hectic at the time, I would try. Trying, however, only found me in my new Lutheran church on sporadic Sunday mornings, but it was a start. I would attend, Jonathan on my lap and as I listened to the sermons, songs and fellowship, felt I was doing a great thing for Jonathan. I sensed an odd and very strong pull to make sure he grew up knowing God. Sporadic Sundays aside, we would leave the church when we moved from the Washington, DC area to Northern Mississippi and God took a back seat to settling in, work and life in general. He still pulled at my soul though, and constantly told me I needed to get not only my son, but also myself to church. I could not describe it any other way than to say the calling got louder and louder, so I listened and joined the small Lutheran church in my Mississippi town. My in-laws would become members as well, and each Sunday found Jonathan and me in attendance. The usual congregation count for Sunday worship services was around forty or so members, but I actually found this a positive aspect at first. The larger Lutheran church before the move had hundreds in attendance and the entire service felt like one giant, choreographed performance. When service was over I felt only as if I had fulfilled my required duty and took nothing of God's word home with me. There in that smaller church, however, it was so much more intimate and I found that I wanted to be there with Jonathan. God had told me time and time again that I might want to get to know him better, and although I did not understand why at the time, I would start my journey towards God in that little church for years to come.

The floor dropped out from under my feet on that very sorrowful morning when my beautiful son Jonathan passed away. I was devastated, as any father or mother would be, and angry with God. I was confused and shaken in my faith, not sure if being called to the church had done me any good. Of course, He put me in that church early, and tried time and again to get me to stay and learn more of Him. Then, when I needed Him the most, my urge to repress my grief kept me from everything I actually needed to begin the journey towards wholeness and healing. Through God's grace, however, Jonathan would return to me in spirit and grief would come. Together he and our Father would begin to guide me on my path. Today, I fully understand that God is everywhere, both inside and outside the church, as well as in my own spirit. Yet, during those years of church attendance that led up to my son's passing, being in His house was merely a duty, or something I felt I needed to do for my son. After Jonathan passed and later revealed his spirit to me in the shower, the veil of ego, pride, and arrogance was lifted to uncover my true connection to our Almighty Father. I found a reverence, accepted Jesus as my Savior, and found an inner faith in the Holy Spirit that kept me from going down the wrong path once again.

As grieving fathers, we all have heard good intentioned folks who certainly mean well, but ask questions we would much rather not hear after our loss. For me, I would frequently hear, "How do you make it through that?" The first time I heard that question my response came quickly, instinctively and honestly from my soul, "Through my faith in God." I simply have no idea today how anyone could ever go through the devastation of losing a child without the faith of the Lord. I am delighted in the fact I did not have to find out what it would have been like without his spirit inside of me. God was not done with me yet, though. I found enough faith in Him to make it through the biggest tragedy of my life, but He had so much more to teach me about His plans for me. As I would develop my personal relationship with the Father, I would also come to understand that Jonathan, too, had a personal relationship. Although I never wanted him to go, I take comfort in the belief that on his arrival at God's side, He shared the greater plan with my child, and Jonathan understood. I know this to be true, as when Jonathan comes to me, I can feel he is truly at peace. In turn, that gives me immeasurable comfort.

The Return to Spirit

*"He travels with whoever looks for Him, and
having taken the seeker by the hand, He arouses
him to go in search of himself."*

~ *Al-Ansari*

I stood in the jets of hot water and wondered to myself if the sawdust that blasted from almost every inch of my body would one day finally clog the shower drain. It was Sunday morning and as usual, I had woken early and spent a few quiet hours in the shop doing my crafts. As I continued to heal, I no longer needed a diversion for my mind or ego, and woodwork had become a true hobby I enjoyed when I could. The time for church neared, however, which meant I needed to hose down. As I placed my head directly in the stream's line of fire, Jonathan, as he often does, entered my thoughts. That cleansing, isolated corner of the house had become a sanctuary where I could relate all my insights or emotions with him I so desired. That morning I silently shared my thoughts and blessing for coming to a better understanding with not only God, but His son, Jesus Christ, and the Holy Spirit as well. I had wanted to know the greater plan, as it were, and that morning I related to Jonathan my joy for finding a little. Like many men who have lived through a tragic and catastrophic event, acceptance of the loss is one thing, but to know the ultimate answer of why becomes an insatiable yearning. While everything just seemed so hard to comprehend immediately after the loss, the one true, fundamental understanding I possessed was my faith that God existed. He had always been with me, although throughout the majority of my life I had chosen not to acknowledge His presence. However, I knew that at every point in my past when I felt the bottom had dropped out, God was the one who pushed my spirit upwards and placed me back on a sound track.

There in the shower I thought back to the morning I held my precious child in my arms while he took his final breath. I remembered being almost entirely in the hospital bed with Jonathan when the doctor placed an empathetic hand on my shoulder as she softly told me there was nothing else that could be done. She backed quietly away several feet and left me alone to be with my son. I had not given up at that point, though. I pushed the tears back for a moment and quietly at first urged Jonathan to fight and come back to me. My voice and desperation would raise as I pleaded repeatedly for him to remember how many times in his life he had fought and won. I would beg until the tears took over and I began to sob uncontrollably, not concerned about the dozens of medical staff in the room. I had suddenly become aware of their remaining presence, as they had somberly moved back to the walls around the room. Up until that point, I had failed to recognize that those amazing, dedicated men and woman who tried valiantly to revive Jonathan's failed heart had not just walked out of the room. I looked up for a moment and scanned about, only to notice that many wept along with me as I anguished over my child. Their compassionate reaction actually gave me a little shot of hope and determination, so once again, I begged my child to fight just one last time for Daddy. He had to fight to show those people in the room just how strong he really was. In my pleading, I fully expected my little angel to open his eyes and the silent machines that had monitored his vital stats to come back on to the surprise of all.

Those damned monitors, which had annoyed me so often over the years, would not come back on line, though. I would have given the world to hear the sweet music of those maddening blips and beeps again that morning. Yet, my dear child, so full of love and innocence was taken from me shortly after dawn and the monitors remained silent. I had no choice but to slowly come to the unbelievable realization that he was gone. He would not again open those beautiful, soft blue eyes he had inherited from my father. When the unavoidable grasp that he was gone came over me, I found all I could do at the moment was stare at his still flush face and repeat over and over again, "Oh, my sweet, sweet baby. I am so sorry." As I ran my fingers lightly through his soft, brown hair, I placed my nose against his soft cheek and whispered tenderly, "Jon-Jon. Daddy will see you again, baby. It won't be soon for me but we will be together again." I was not sure at the time where those words came from. They might not seem so deep to some but the moments they passed from my lips they vibrated so deeply and through to my very core.

How could I say those words, though? That child was my love and my life. His birth, along with his struggles and his triumphs since he came in to the world with such an incredible challenge had changed me as I had watched him grow. I went from a lifestyle of no concern or commitment for others to the father of a miracle child. His inner strength and fortitude was everything I wanted to be and through him, I had secretly tried to inherit his virtues. Was I not supposed to be devastatingly insane with his loss and scream out that I just could never live without him? Should I not have wondered how I would go on with my own life? I felt something, however, and it was strong. It was God and His Holy Spirit that wanted to live in me, but I did not know it at the time. The bottom had dropped out of my life again, and as always before, God had a hand on my soul. I would not come to the realization that God was always with me until that fateful morning so many months later when I allowed myself to grieve in the shower. When Jonathan's sweet spirit moved through me that morning, I finished my shower a new child of God and set off to attempt a greater understanding of His spirit.

I had struggled greatly with the decision to share my views of faith, since the belief in the Creator is such a personal and individual issue. I was concerned that my own beliefs and discoveries might actually isolate or offend other grieving fathers. If offended by my ideologies, would another man give no credence to my healing journey either, based on the notion that I did not believe in a certain discipline, dogma, or concept? I certainly do not judge any other for individual beliefs or practices, and to this day stand by my certainty that it is only necessary to believe in the one Creator. It is a personal decision how one chooses to practice that belief. It was actually during one of my more recent shower sojourns that I would come to the decision that I would share my own beliefs, for if I did not, I would not be true to myself or to Jonathan in my writings. Although I did not recognize God was always in my heart, I was raised with a conviction that He existed, along with a Heaven, Hell, and Lucifer. Up until the age of eight or so, I would be taken to the neighborhood Southern Baptist church where I attended Sunday school in the church basement while my mother would attend services upstairs. I recall the childhood books on Jesus and his miracles, the playtime in the open fields with other kids, and the question of whether I would like to attend services upstairs one day. Somewhere along the way, and through whom I do not recall, my desire to attend services would be snuffed out by both fear of the church and of God Himself. I had been given the impression that what took place above my Sunday school sessions was led by a very angry man who yelled frequently, called everyone a sinner, and claimed God was an angry God who would send them all to Hell. As a young child, all I knew was that the easiest way not to go to Hell was to avoid the angry man in the church and the angrier man in Heaven. At about the same time my father, who worked every day except Sunday, had just gotten a new fishing boat and Sunday was the only day he could enjoy it. If I would do my duty each Saturday night by catching a can full of nightcrawlers, I could be his fishing friend on Sunday mornings and avoid the bad man at church altogether. Many Saturday nights to come would find me in the yard with a coffee can and a flashlight, and just as soon as the dew would hit the lawn, the worms came up and gave me my ticket out of church. When Sunday fishing faded away with the change of seasons, I

balked at the thought of Sunday school and soon I was no longer
pressured in to going at all. For me, God was an angry God who spoke
through that man in the church.

While I would not try to imply the short stint in Sunday school
alone gave me a strong faith, thankfully, life in general back then
certainly did. Life in the sixties was filled with heavy religious
undertones that at least gave me some idea He was all around. God,
prayer, and the Pledge of Allegiance were still prevalent in my schools,
as it was in many of the community activities, such as little league ball,
scouting and so much more. The Christmas holidays would be filled
with wonderful movies and television specials featuring angels and
wise men, while carols sung brought visions of the baby Jesus, Silent
Night and the Little Drummer Boy. I put together my own
understanding that God was the angry creator and Jesus was his good
son. As I aged I had absolutely zero knowledge of the various organized
religions, and frankly, with the pack of no-gooders I ran with in my
young teens, I rarely ventured near a church, except for the occasional
family wedding or late night opportunity to park in a dark corner of the
lot and make out with my girl. It would not be until I entered Marine
Corps Boot Camp that I first discovered there were different religions
when on day two I was issued my Dog Tags. Along with my name,
branch of service, social security number, and blood type stamped into
the metal was the word Protestant. I had no idea what Protestant was
or what it meant. I received a clue, however, on the first Sunday when
after morning PT, or physical training, followed by chow and then more
PT, the Drill Instructor announced that it was time for the Sunday

services. He went on to say that anyone who wished to be a wimp could have an hour at the "Magic Show" while the non-believers could scrub the squad bay deck to keep busy. I did not care much for church, but cared more than the thought of scrubbing the barracks floor for an hour, as did the remainder of my squad. The threat of scrubbing only insured the Drill Instructor got an hour alone on what would become a quiet Sunday morning for him. When he barked out instructions for the Catholics to form one line and the Protestants another, a quick mental equation in my mind told me that Protestant must be a special military word for Baptist. I had put that down as my religious preference when I had enlisted, as all I knew was the Baptist church from my youth. So, I would "snap-to" in the Protestant line, be marched in formation to church services and wondered if an angry man would tell me I was going straight to Hell.

After Boot Camp, I would have no real calling to attend church and know God better until well after Jonathan was born. While it would be a slow, mild pull at my stubborn soul, I felt the desire was due to what I had witnessed in the seemingly God given miracles during Jonathan's past hospital stays. The Pastor mysteriously appeared when needed and prayed for the people and actions that I felt had actually saved my child. Later in life, I would come to understand that there are no coincidences, but even back then, I knew God had His hand in caring for my son. My simple mindset at the time was at least I needed to give some type of payback or thanks to God. Thus, I would become a member of the Lutheran church there in Springfield, Virginia but attended very infrequently, as the church was moderately large and I felt completely out of place. With my lack of a religious foundation, each Sunday felt more as if I had attended a play in which I arrived mid-way through the performance. I had no real idea who the characters were, nor was I aware of the story line really. Because of that, attendance for me would become a duty instead of a soul satisfying joy. I would leave each visit of the church having felt as if I had satisfied some religious check off box just for having made it there. When I would eventually move from the suburbs of Washington, DC and found a home in Northern Mississippi, it would take a few years before God would tug at my soul again. When he did, I found and joined a small, local Lutheran church in our community where Jonathan and I would attend a series of new member classes together. I was actually astonished and very pleased to hear my son, who was somewhat shy around new adults, as he responded well and demonstrated a good understanding of faith. He seemed actually further down the road than I did. I paid attention, though, and took great pleasure in the lessons, which talked of the various organized religions and the differing rites and practices of many. That understanding seemed to fill one gap I had had in my bag of God knowledge up to that point in my adult life.

Jonathan and I would attend Sunday services on a regular basis and participated in many of the church events, such as puppet shows, car washes, and the ever-popular potluck dinners. Eventually he and I took over the fun responsibility of the church sound system and as a father-son team spent our Sunday mornings side by side in front of the mixer board. As buddies, we manipulated microphones on queue and adjusted volume levels and felt like the building was under our command. We looked forward to Sunday mornings so much, where we would enjoy the time we worked together like two good friends. There was an additional benefit as well. Before the morning service would begin, Jonathan and I did an early review of the service program in order to make notes as to where microphones would be turned on and off throughout the morning. By doing so, we had an early perusal of the day's Gospel readings, the sermon topic, as well as the scriptures that would be offered to the congregation in various readings. Out of necessity, we went over these in detail and then out of desire we discussed the teachings together before the service started. Through these little one-on-one readings, I would come to experience a little higher level of understanding for religion and developed a desire to know more. Surely, I thought, the way to understand God and religion was to study the Bible, so it seemed obvious that I should join the men's Bible study group. Sadly, I got very little satisfaction from the classes, as once again I felt somewhat out of place. At the time I had joined, the men were deep somewhere within the New Testament and I felt like a third grade student in math class who had just been handed a book on advanced trigonometry. I quickly became discouraged and dropped out of the Bible study, satisfied that possibly I could catch up after years and years of upcoming attendance.

Suddenly, the unimaginable happened and I lost my sweet Jonathan when his precious but delicate heart failed. I continued to attend church every Sunday, but for the most part really had no desire to be there. I was not sure how it could help my loss, or even where it would lead, so instead of worshipping God, I took umbrage to everything that was preached. For so many Sundays, I would listen to readings of the Gospel that spoke of God's love and be silently indignant. All those words in the Bible sounded great for everyone else, but what about me? Where was God's love for me? How could my tragedy happen when I had followed God's calling and brought my son and myself into the church each week before he passed? What I listened to each Sunday seemed like just words used to make others who had not experienced my pain feel better about their normal day to day lives. Sermons, lessens, psalms were all the same. Each referred to a God who was not concerned about me. Yet, it was my duty to attend. I had become a member of that little Lutheran church long before my loss, and without question, nearly every member unselfishly took some part in sending Jonathan off beautifully. Because of their commitment to me, I would attend out of respect for the church, but I did not want to be there.

Then, as I have mentioned so often, life and my faith would change when on a fateful morning, grief was allowed to come and I cried in the shower. Almost immediately, I understood the loss was not just about me at all. Sure, nothing would ever take away the emptiness and pain I felt inside, but I instantly had a reconfirmation of my core belief that I was so much more than just a mind that functioned only to drive a physical body around in daily life. I knew I had a powerful, intelligent spirit that dwelled inside my physical presence and yes, that spirit came only from God. That spirit would not and could not cease to exist when the body gave way. Nor would Jonathan's, as I knew his spirit still endured and was doing whatever he was meant to do when not present with me here on earth. We are all our own spirit, made by God the Father, and once we accept His son Jesus Christ as our savior, the Holy Spirit becomes one with our own. It is my core belief that this is where the Holy Trinity comes in. With me, I believed in the Father, yet thought so little of the Son. When I would accept Jesus Christ as my Savior, along with his unconditional love, the Holy Spirit joined with mine and I was suddenly connected to God, and wonderfully through him, my child.

As a grieving father, I took enormous comfort in knowing Jonathan was, above all else, his own spirit and child of God. With that, I cannot help but take great honor from the knowledge that both he and God entrusted me to be a major part of his life for the short time he was here. I do not ask that anyone accept my personal interpretations of the Bible or my beliefs in the Holy Trinity, although I know I share those thoughts with so many. However, I begrudge no other believer or non-believer, and remain committed to respect the views, rites, and ceremonies of those who worship in whatever manner they so choose, as long as it harms no one. I ask only that others pay the same respect of me, as here I seek only to relate that my beliefs in a higher power have given me incredible healing and an understanding that there is so much more to life beyond yesterday and today. For the most part, I will admit selfishness, as the loss of my son continues to bring an emptiness to my heart that will never be filled. I sometimes let that get beyond the fact that I should feel even greater sorrow for my child, who was taken before he truly had a chance to enjoy the beauty of life. He had his own spirit, though, granted by God and whether his journey on earth from start to finish was known to him before he came is unknown to me. It is written that only God knows the number of our days. Yet, I like knowing that Jonathan had his own journey to travel, and under his own terms, as well. I feel incredibly humbled and blessed to have been a part of his life for the short time I had him in mine. His spirit still exists, though, and I know you too can feel the spirit of your own lost child every day. If you are so inclined to know why, as I was, I do hope you find an understanding for that feeling. It is the presence of your child. It is his or her spirit surrounding you, and may be so much easier to feel when seen through a connection with God. Our spirit will never cease either, and as I get closer to the golden ages, am comforted in knowing who will greet me when I return home and see my beautiful Jonathan Taylor Kelly again.

I am on the journey of wholeness and healing, and I pray you are as well. Perhaps, like me, you do not want nor expect to heal completely. Yet, we must hold to the certainty, without question or doubt, that if we remain strong in our faith we will hold our child again. It will be a blink of an eye for that baby that misses us as much as we miss him or her, yet feel like a thousand lifetimes in our hearts. Until then, may you find peace on earth in your child's eternal spirit and unconditional love. That feeling inside is meant for you and is given only by your little angel. Take it and live an incredible life knowing love surrounds you, although sometimes unseen! Neither spirit nor love has an end.

Acknowledgements

Without question, I give tribute for this publication to the legacy left behind by my loving son, Jonathan. Without him, my heart could not be as enriched as it is and I may never have experienced true, unconditional love.

Yet, without the dedicated men and women in the medical field, I would have never had the chance to know my child for the short time I had him. Those selfless doctors, nurses, and other support staff deal not only with life and loss, but with human emotions as well. We deservedly thank those in uniform for their service to country and community but may forsake those who, often in the grimmest of times, have become some of the greatest heroes in my life.

If only God knows the number of our days, He truly chooses only those with the purest devotion, desire, and talent to hold onto the poor ill or injured souls whose time has not come...and the compassionate heart to handle those whose time has. Incredible people gave me sixteen and a half years more than I could have had with my loving child, and I shall always acknowledge that gift.

About the Author

R. Glenn Kelly, grieving and healing father of Jonathan Taylor Kelly, has written professionally throughout his adult life. He has composed many informative articles published within trade periodicals in various industries and authored numerous award-winning responses to federal government solicitations in the defense industry, as well. With graphic arts as another passion, R. Glenn has also designed attractive print media ads and marketing materials for numerous companies along the way. An avid public speaker, he is just as much at home talking to an audience as he is conversing with friends over dinner.

To find out more, or to contact R. Glenn directly, please visit www.grievingmen.com, where you are invited to share or join in discussions related to the journey of all men who have suffered loss. R. Glenn is enthusiastically available for speaking engagements, grief workshop participation or in other ways he might serve others who have lost a loved one. He can be contacted through email directly at rglennkelly@rglennkelly.com.

"The best way to find yourself is to lose yourself in the service of others."
~ Mahatma Gandhi